D1567777

THE MILITARY ARCHIVES

First published 2022 by Eastwood Books

Dublin, Ireland
www.eastwoodbooks.com
www.wordwellbooks.com

First edition

Eastwood Books is an imprint of the Wordwell Group

Eastwood Books
The Wordwell Group
Unit 9, 78 Furze Road
Sandyford
Dublin, Ireland

ISBN: 978-1-913934-33-0 (Hardback)
ISBN: 978-1-913934-43-9 (Ebook)

British Library Cataloguing in Publication Data.
A catalogue record for this book is available from the National Library of Ireland and
the British Library.

Copyediting by Conor Reidy
Layout and design by Wordwell
Printed in Poland by L&C Printing Group

THE MILITARY ARCHIVES

A HISTORY

Daniel Ayiotis

EASTWOOD BOOKS

Dedicated to the memory of my Father-in-Law,
Jim Tobin (1953–2022).
One of life's true gentlemen. I know how much
you'd have loved to have seen the book.

CONTENTS

Acknowledgements   vii

Foreword   ix

Introduction   xiii

Prologue   1922–1924: Piaras Béaslaí and the Seeds of the Military Archives   xxi

Chapter 1   1924–1926: The Military Archives Established   1

Chapter 2   1926–1932: The Military Archives Stagnates   32

Chapter 3   1933–1935: Colonel EV O'Carroll and the Anglo-Irish Conflict Project   42

Chapter 4   1935–1976: Rise and Fall – The Colonel JJ 'Ginger' O'Connell Years and After   57

Chapter 5   1976–1990: The Commandant Peter Young Years (Part 1)   85

Chapter 6   1991–1999: The Commandant Peter Young Years (Part 2)   112

Chapter 7   1999–2012: The Commandant Victor
             Laing Years   131

Chapter 8   2012–2016: The Modern Military Archives   145

Epilogue   The Present   152

Notes   158

Index   170

ACKNOWLEDGEMENTS

I am extremely privileged to be in my position as the Military Archives' director and to be surrounded by the people that I am, on a daily basis. First and foremost, my military and civilian team-mates have given me tremendous support in this endeavour to tell the story of an institution about which we care so sincerely. This assistance has not just taken the form of research assistance and the benefit of their depth of experience and knowledge, but through conversations, memories, reminisces and even throw-away remarks. Many times, you were contributing to this book without even knowing it. For this, I want to express my eternal gratitude to Archivists Hugh Beckett, Lisa Dolan, Noelle Grothier and Linda Hickey. Huge thanks are due to the military staff who keep the Archives running day to day, both those currently posted here and those who retired or transferred during the time that I have been researching and writing this book - Company Quartermaster Tom Mitchell, Sergeants David 'Ned' Kelly and Matthew Weafer, Corporals Kevin Byrne and Joseph McDermott. as well as to our volunteers Lieutenant Colonel Richard Cummins (retired), Colonel Tom Hodson (retired), Tony Kinsella, Sergeant Gerry McCann (retired), Denis McCarthy, and Flight Sergeant James Perkins (retired). Thanks are also due to senior archivist and *Military Service Pensions Collection* Project Manager Cécile Chemin and her team, Robert McEvoy, Michael Keane, Sam McGrath, Leanne Ledwidge and the team of digitisation technicians from Mallon Technology. Thanks also to former Officers-in-Charge of the Military Archives Commandant Victor Laing (retired), Lieutenant Colonel Padraic Kennedy, Commandant Stephen Mac Eoin, and Commandant Claire Mortimer, and to Commandant Billy Campbell (retired), Commandant Pat Brennan (retired), and Colonel Stephen Ryan.

I owe a debt of gratitude to many people outside of my own organisation, in particular Dr Michael Kennedy, Dr Catriona Crowe, Dr Robert Fisk (RIP), Professor Eunan O'Halpin, Dr Eoin Kinsella, Dr Pat McCarthy and Dominic Price. Special thanks to Dr Eve Morrison for her generosity in sharing her research into the Bureau of Military History.

Many thanks to all those who shared their memories, stories and experiences of Commandant Peter Young, 'the Father of the Military Archives.' It is not often that you hear someone remembered so fondly, without exception, by so many. Acknowledgement and thanks are in fact due to Peter Young himself, for all of the reasons covered in the two chapters of this book dedicated to his tenure.

Finally, sincere thanks are due to my wife, Victoria, for her unrelenting love, support and encouragement.

FOREWORD

'Vision, perseverance and commitment'[1]

In this lively, engaging and authoritative history of Ireland's Military Archives, Commandant Daniel Ayiotis skilfully explores how the institution developed out of the vision almost a century ago of a handful of far-sighted military and civilians. That small visionary group saw the need to preserve Ireland's military records. They gave their vision form in what has become today's outward-facing and internationally-renowned Military Archives, the place of deposit for records relating to the Defence Forces and the Department of Defence.

After 1922, the passing decades brought plans to develop a proper Military Archives. The 1920s saw remarkable schemes put forward by Colonel Michael J. Costello and the prescient and foresighted Thomas Galvin to create an archive linked to the immediate needs of Ireland's military forces and that would eventually become a resource for historians. This is notable in a decade where professional history was in its infancy in Ireland and many of the pre-1922 records of the country were lost in the destruction of the Public Records Office during the civil war.

Ireland's military posture is a result of its geopolitical location, and the requirements of future defence can be gleaned by astute analysis of past actions. The Defence Forces need their archives as a basic military intelligence source. It is a guide to how the past defence of the state has future relevance. Civilian researchers might forget, or more likely are unaware, that an archive can be a strong military asset. The military purpose of maintaining proper archives emerges strongly from the pages below.

Without access to the records in an archive it is not possible to write evidence-based history. An archive is thus a most powerful place. Command of it is a strategically important role. And while Daniel correctly makes it clear that the archives are not just for historians (despite what many historians might think!) the archive is the place where history is made. The records it holds are not a passive body of material. Controlling history via control of those records can be a way to seek to protect reputations in the present and direct opinions into the future. Interrogating the archive allows narratives to be checked, corrected and written anew. As Daniel puts it, and as the actions of Piaras Béaslaí and Éamon de Valera amongst others in the opening chapters show, the Military Archives has been a 'contested space, characterised by competing narratives'. Its very contents, the records themselves, are alive.

At times the people of Ireland have shown a remarkable willingness to capture their history. The loss of the Public Records Office in 1922 in large part gave the impetus to the formation of the Irish Manuscripts Commission in 1928. The Bureau of Military History, established almost two decades later was another venture undertaken with foresight and vision. Yet, despite these great ventures, Military Archives was at the same time run down for a variety of bureaucratic, security, political, financial, human and anti-intellectual reasons. Post-war, in the 1958 re-organisation of the Defence Forces, Military Archives was taken off the establishment and languished. What Ayiotis succinctly terms 'enduring neglect' was the norm for the following quarter of a century.

In the early-1980s, the actions of Commandant Peter Young ensured that, in the unmistakable words of Denis McCarthy 'Vague rumours about an elusive Military Archives began to take concrete form, and it transpired that once upon a time such a body had come briefly into existence, and was in the process of slowly being resuscitated.' Peter Young ensured that the patient, though recuperating in harsh surroundings and with the bare minimum of resources to aid them, was on the road to recovery and was, as Daniel succinctly puts it 'gaining momentum'. Dr Pat McCarthy's remark that Peter was 'a guy who came up with an idea, and then went and delivered on it' is right on the mark. Commandant Peter Young singlehandedly saved Military Archives. It is an education in human endeavour reading Daniel's account of how this came about through Peter's willpower and cleverness.

Commandant Victor Laing held the line at Military Archives through the critical period following Peter Young's all too early death in 1999 and began to implement plans for future expansion. Victor's achievements allowed his successors Commandant Stephen MacEoin and Commandant Padraic Kennedy gain the necessary impetus, using the leverage of the Decade of Centenaries, to enable the release of the Bureau of Military History Records and the Military Service Pensions Collection. They also gave Military Archives a real web presence as both collections went online free to access in cyberspace.

Today Military Archives is, as Daniel says in his epilogue, 'a mature and confident institution.' In exploring its history, he has shown, to quote President Michael D. Higgins on the opening of the Military Archive's new premises in Cathal Brugha Barracks, Dublin in April 2016, 'the fundamental importance of the Military Archives towards our understanding of the founding events of the state' and indeed, of the century that has followed.

Shortly after he took over command of Military Archives, Daniel said to me that his mission was 'to make information available' and he has often said to me that the Defence Forces needs to 'own its history', not shy away from it. Readers of his outstanding account will see how, with this book he has now pushed his mission forward into new dimensions on both these fronts. He has shown the fundamental importance of safeguarding the history of the Defence Forces and the value, for soldier and civilian alike, of using its archives to engage with military perspectives in understanding the national and international history of independent Ireland.

Michael Kennedy

INTRODUCTION

Around 2008, when I was a young lieutenant based in Aiken Barracks, Dundalk, I would hear other officers talking about a captain who had taken the eccentric step of seeking a posting at a place called 'The Military Archives' in Cathal Brugha Barracks, Rathmines. *Your man who'd opted out of his career*, as some described him. For my own part, I had never heard of the enigmatic Military Archives prior to this time. As a junior infantry officer, busily involved with training recruits, battalion exercises, courses, regimental duties and generally trying to stay out of trouble and with a good eighty kilometres of the M1 motorway safely separating me from the machinations of the Brigade Headquarters in Cathal Brugha Barracks, such a place at the Military Archives was well beyond my horizon. It conjured images in my mind of this captain sitting in dimly lit Dickensian surroundings, at a large oak desk, poring over dusty old pages by candlelight, occasionally making notes in a ledger with a quill and ink.

This captain was Stephen Mac Eoin. Little did I know that by 2015, I would be based at the Military Archives myself, in the same Staff Officer appointment that he then held. Even less did it cross my mind that by 2017, I would take over from him as the Officer-in-Charge of that institution. Life's journey is interesting that way.

Fortunately, Stephen continues to enjoy a successful career. As I write, on top of his normal duties with 3 Infantry Battalion in Kilkenny, he is the chairman of the board established to oversee the Defence Forces'

2022 centenary commemorative programme, a task for which he was personally selected by the Defence Forces Chief of Staff. However, while the wider preconceptions and my own cartoonish misconceptions of the mid- to late-2000s are laughable in hindsight, they were not unfounded either. For a long time, a posting at the Military Archives was considered detrimental to an army officer's career. Officers were, and still are, expected to bounce between command and staff appointments, preferably with experience at Brigade or Defence Forces Headquarters, every few years, building up a broad, strategic knowledge and skills base to have the necessary CV for promotion and advancement. The Military Archives was traditionally not regarded as a desirable posting in this respect. NCOs and private soldiers based there were generally those who were coming to the end of their career or who were not looking to advance any further through the ranks.

Stephen's appointment marked a time of change. Since the reactivation of the Military Archives in 1982 (it had been dormant since the 1940s and removed from the official establishment of the Defence Forces in 1959) there had only been two Officers-in-Charge – Commandant Peter Young from 1982 until 1999 and Commandant Victor Laing from 1999 until 2012. The Archives was an anomaly within the Defence Forces in many ways. While a posting there was not seen as desirable within the wider organisation, the records in its custody were unique and of tremendous national significance. Aside from the *Bureau of Military History*, which contains 1,773 witness statements from an array of people who were involved with the Irish revolutionary period, the Archives holds valuable records from the foundation of the National Army, the Civil War and the Emergency period to highlight just a few. Furthermore, it was a job that required long-term commitment from those who chose to undertake it. It required accumulating substantial institutional knowledge and developing a wide network among the country's cultural, heritage and academic institutions. Being understaffed and under-resourced, it also placed a very substantial workload on the officers, NCOs and privates who worked there. Most crucially, is required a genuine love for the work. It has always been a vocation.

In 2006, to mark the ninetieth anniversary of the 1916 Easter Rising, the Taoiseach, Bertie Ahern, announced that the military service pension files relating to Ireland's revolutionary period from 1916-1923 would be released into the public domain for the centenary of the Rising the following decade. This single government decision initiated the momentum that would build to the release of not just the *Military Service (1916-1923) Pensions Collection* but greater professionalisation, increased budgets, the hiring of civilian archivists and, ultimately, the construction of the Military Archives' current facility at Cathal Brugha Barracks. Stephen Mac Eoin was the first 'early career' officer to get involved with what was becoming a much more dynamic establishment, both within the Defence Forces and among the state's heritage institutions. His appointment – and that it could attract a young army officer with the foresight to see where it was going – heralded the sea change to come.

I came to the Military Archives entirely through serendipity. I joined the 79th Cadet Class in 2002 and in 2004 was commissioned as a second lieutenant to 27 Infantry Battalion, based between Aiken Barracks, Dundalk and the now closed Monaghan Military Barracks. Battalion life was interesting and varied. Between 2005 and 2008, I spent the college semesters as a full-time student at the National University of Ireland, Galway. This was the normal progression, that young officers who did not have one already would earn an undergraduate degree – primarily at the National University of Ireland, Galway or the Galway-Mayo Institute of Technology. I studied Sociology and Politics, and Philosophy, attaining my BA in 2008. While I could have studied something with a more obvious correlation to the work of the Army – engineering, science, languages etc. – it is a background that has stood to me greatly as an archivist. I am adamant that a grounding in social and political science, and philosophy, are as relevant, or even more relevant, to proper engagement with archival work than an educational background in history. The role of an archive within a state is not simply to provide historical curiosities, to help genealogists track down ancestors or to supply raw materials to the burgeoning Irish history book market. The role of an archive is accountability of the state and advocacy for the citizens of the state, through the provision of access to the documentary evidence of decisions made on their behalf by their governments and other state agencies. Once you understand that, it is clear why some understanding of how societies function, of theories of government, ethics, and knowledge, form a solid bedrock for archival work. I did not appreciate this at the time of course. I just found them interesting.

With tours of duty to Kosovo and Lebanon under my belt, as well as a variety of command and staff officer appointments, by 2013, I was a captain and had served just over nine years with 27Infantry Battalion. One afternoon, I was called into the office of my Commanding Officer, Lieutenant Colonel Maureen O'Brien (who would go on to be the Defence Forces' first female general), and informed that I was to report to Cathal Brugha Barracks with immediate effect. Word had arrived from the Brigade Adjutant, completely out of the blue to the both of us, that I had been transferred to a logistical appointment in 2 Brigade Ordnance Group, as the Ordnance Supply Platoon Commander.

2 Brigade Ordnance Group was completely different to battalion life. The NCOs were great and I had a lot more independence in my work. The thing was, the NCOs were a bit *too* great. The Ordnance Supply Platoon had been newly established during the previous reorganisation of the Defence Forces to replace the Logistical Supply Battalion (LSB) and many of the NCOs were handpicked for their experience and diligence. This meant that the place basically ran itself, which led to my own job, which was entirely administrative, not being the most stimulating. To keep my myself challenged and entertained, I ended up establishing and running an experimental performance event called Mixed Messages with the woman who I would eventually marry. Again, expanding my interest in the arts and that whole area, while not an obvious bedfellow for a military career, would later prove useful. There are innumerable opportunities for creative collaborations and artistic residencies within the heritage institutions, not least the Military Archives. Archiving is

an interdisciplinary pursuit, and the historian's lens is only one of many through which we can engage with our documentary and evidential heritage. Again, I did not realise this at the time, but the various threads were beginning to converge. Simultaneously, through other social circles, I was extending my associations with various veterans' groups and developing that network too. Again, this was with no particular aim in mind besides the fact that I found it interesting.

By 2015, I was considering moving on from the Army. I even had a ludicrous idea at one stage about trying to run performance events and open mics on a full-time basis. Thankfully my wife, Victoria, talked sense into me. With her encouragement, I booked some career coaching sessions with a friend of ours, the astute and wise Anne Tannam, who we knew through the writing group at which Victoria and I had met. The result was a renewed appreciation of all of the factors that had attracted me to an army career in the first place, with a new emphasis on finding an appointment within the organisation that would re-enthuse me.

As if by magic, it was very soon afterwards that I saw a position for a Staff Officer at the Military Archives advertised in the barracks. It piqued my interest. It would have piqued my interest had I still been based in Dundalk too but being in that general milieu of Cathal Brugha Barracks meant that it was easier to find out more in a casual way. Being based there meant that I could wander over to the mess at coffee time to suss it out, or to informally chat and find out more from the people involved. So, I applied and sat the interview around March of 2015.

Just like that, life's various threads converged at a single point, and I got the job. And I've loved every minute of it.

The idea of writing a book about the Military Archives developed as I gained more familiarity with the place and realised that it dated back to the beginning of the Defence Forces itself. My starting point was the first two lines of the administrative and biographical history of the *Historical Section Collection* descriptive catalogue, written by archivist Lisa Dolan:

The first establishment of a Military Archives, also known for a period as the Historical Section, operated as a sub section of Army Headquarters Intelligence from the earliest period of the Defence Forces until 1959. The genesis of this section may be connected to the activities of Commandant General Piaras Béaslaí and Captain JJ Burke who acquired and managed records during the Civil War years.

It all grew from there. The more I researched, the more I realised how rich a history the Military Archives has. But what form would it take?

At one brief stage I considered using the topic as the basis for a PhD dissertation but decided against it just as quickly. I wanted this project to be a labour of love. I wanted to retain creative control but also, since the Military Archives constitutes a significant aspect of my life, I did not want to grow to resent the project. I still wanted the book to be well researched and referenced and I hope that I have achieved this. But I did not want it to be an 'academic' book either. So many people have recently become aware of the important records held at the Military Archives, particularly during the *Decade of Centenaries*, but many do not know the story of the institution itself or how those records came to be in our custody. I also wanted the freedom to be able to occasionally duck down little side streets and dedicate some of the wordcount to biographical sketches or anecdotes of some of the key players in the Archives' story. The Military Archives did not develop in a vacuum but within the broader context of the formation and evolution of the Defence Forces and the Irish State, and was, therefore, subject to the various political and social vagaries and exigencies as the rest of the Defence Forces and the country. Many of the players, those centre stage, those in supporting roles and those who make cameo appearances, played roles on the national stage too. I am sure many of the names within will be familiar.

What I hope I have achieved is an informed, accessible and interesting story about an institution that I personally find fascinating, told through a combination of the events, the decisions and the people that made it what it is today. It is not an almanac, a state gazette, an index or a reference encyclopaedia of the Military Archives. I know I have neglected to mention people who have been involved with the Military Archives directly and indirectly over the years, particularly in later years where people came and went through short term postings or attachments or as volunteers, interns, or project archivists. So, to any of those people whose names do not appear within, please accept my apologies in advance. It is not intended as a denigration of your contribution to the Miliary Archives. I am also aware that in the latter half of the book, when the chronology of events reaches current living memory, that I have had to occasionally be judicious with sensitive sources and paraphrase without citation, or simply left less pertinent aspects out, either as a matter of common courtesy to people still living or to keep the narrative flowing.

With all that said, I have thoroughly enjoyed researching and writing this book. Whatever about their assessments of my degree of success, I am sure that my colleagues, past and present, will agree that the story of the Miliary Archives is one worth telling. I hope you do too.

Daniel Ayiotis
February 2022

Prologue

1922–1924: PIARAS BÉASLAÍ AND THE SEEDS OF THE MILITARY ARCHIVES

T he seeds of the Military Archives were sown by Commandant General Piaras Béaslaí and Captain James Joseph 'JJ' Burke, who acquired and managed National Army records during the Civil War years. Béaslaí and Burke, like the officers who would succeed them as influential figures in the development of the Military Archives, had strong revolutionary credentials. Béaslaí had been a member of the Volunteer Executive from its formation in November 1913 until October 1915 and a member of the General Headquarters (GHQ) Staff of the IRA from July 1918 until the foundation of the National Army in early 1922. Holding the rank of Vice-Commandant, as the Second-in-Command of the 1st Battalion of the Dublin Brigade IRA during the 1916 Easter Rising, he saw action at Church Street and the Four Courts. He was imprisoned following the Rising until the amnesty in June 1917 and subsequently incarcerated for periods in 1918 and 1919. From 1919, he was posted to IRA GHQ as the editor of *An tÓglách*, the IRA's newspaper during the War of Independence which later transitioned into a National Army publication with the Civil War and the IRA split. As a journalist in civilian life, Béaslaí was a natural choice for the appointment.

During 1920, Béaslaí held the additional GHQ appointment of Director of Publicity. This role he carried over into the establishment of the National Army in 1922, when he was Director of Army Publicity as well as Chief Military Censor, based at an office in Brunswick Street, Dublin, a position he held from 28 June until 1 December of that year.[1] During the 1919–1923 period, Béaslaí was also a member of the 1st, 2nd and 3rd Dáil Éireann, and in 1922 toured the USA on a publicity campaign in support of the Anglo-Irish Treaty.

JJ Burke came from Ranelagh in Dublin and joined the National Army in July of 1922. Like Béaslaí, Burke was a journalist by profession, initially posted to the Publicity Section and later the Reports and Statistics Branch. Like Béaslaí, Burke had cut his teeth during the revolutionary years. He joined the Irish Volunteers in 1913 and the IRB in 1914 at the invitation of Eamon Ceannt. That same year, while participating in the 'Howth Gun-Running,' he sustained a bayonet wound to his left side from a soldier of the King's Own Scottish Borderers. During the 1916 Easter Rising he fought as a Squad Commander at the South Dublin Union. Beaten, abused, and threatened with death while in custody at Kilmainham, he was sentenced to death, commuted to three-years penal servitude. Following subsequent detention in Portland and Lewes jails he was released under the 1917 amnesty.

Upon his release, Burke re-joined 'A' Company, 4th Battalion, Dublin Brigade IRA. During this time, he also worked on several republican newspapers including *Young Ireland, Nationality, Truth* and *The Irish People*, often as assistant to Arthur Griffith and acting as editor of *Nationality* and *Young Ireland* while Griffith was imprisoned as a result of the 'German Plot' - a bogus conspiracy originating from the British administration in Dublin Castle that the Sinn Féin movement was colluding with the Germans to start an armed insurrection in Ireland. In November 1920, Burke was transferred to the 3rd Battalion and arrested shortly afterwards at the office of Arthur Griffith. He spent a year in Ballykinlar Internment Camp, County Down, joining the National Army shortly after his release.[2]

In October 1922, with the support of the Collins family, Béaslaí was reluctantly extended a request by the government to write the official biography of General Michael Collins. Collins, the Commander-in-Chief of the National Army and a close friend of Béaslaí, was killed less than two months previously in an ambush at Beál na Bláth, County Cork. Béaslaí had in turn sought the assistance of Captain Burke 'for a special job in connection with this project.'[3] Along with Burke, who received an additional £4.0.0. a week from Béaslaí on top of his Army pay for this work, Béaslaí was provided with a typist (Miss G Glendon) whom he paid £2.0.0 a week. Despite the seemingly auspicious start, this project proved to be a contentious one.

By March of 1923, Béaslaí was lamenting the fact that, while he could have written the biography of Collins 'more interesting and inti-mate' on his own, he had 'elected to write the official biography, under Government censorship and with no profit.'[4] General Richard Mulcahy, who had briefly been the Army's Chief of Staff before he succeeded Collins as Commander-in-Chief following his death, had offered Béaslaí release from military duties for this purpose in October 1922, but this did not materialise until March of 1923. As far as Béaslaí was concerned, he had been promised 'every facility' but instead got none, 'save the use of an empty room in the barracks,' even having to provide his own station-ary. Adding insult to injury, having been assured that undertaking this historical literary project would not prejudice his position in the Army, he was instead gazetted into the lower rank of colonel which, given his previous service, he felt 'could only be interpreted by the public as a reflection upon my Army record' and as a suggestion that he had been reduced in rank for doing something wrong. Béaslaí was well aware that he was the only pre-Treaty Commandant General to not be gazetted as Major General in the new Army organisation, and the final indignity was receiving notification that his reduction in rank and pay had been applied retrospectively.

Three months later, in June 1923, shortly after the end of the Civil War, Béaslaí wrote a letter to the Army's Chief of Staff, General Seán

Mac Mahon, in relation to the 'special job' for which he had requested Burke's assistance. In this letter, he requested of Mac Mahon that he:

> Treat the work on which Captain Burke and I are engaged as a temporary Department of Army work, under some such title as War Records. What we are really doing is collecting material and records which would be of great value for reference as a complete history of the Irish Volunteers, IRA, and the starting of the Regular Army, as well as the Anglo-Irish and Irregular Wars. A copy of this material can be filed with the Reports and Statistics Branch, and Captain Burke could be regarded as temporarily on my staff.
>
> When the work of completing the materials is completed (sic) I can then resign my position in the Army, and the Department be wound up. This would be in about two or three months' time, and Captain Burke could then report back to you. I think some such plan would regularise the position as Captain Burke and myself are concerned.[5]

It is clear from this short letter that Béaslaí appreciated the value of this work and recognised the importance of consolidating and preserving the documentary evidence of the newly-formed Irish Army and its roots in the Volunteer movement. This is apparent from the fact that he was, at that time, making plans to retire from the Army but demonstrated an eagerness to finish the job he had started. This motivation, centred firmly on an understanding of the comprehensive and tangible value of a military archive (in spirit if not in name at this early stage) as a strategic asset, would be one common to the officers who would succeed him in the guardianship of Ireland's documentary military heritage.

Béaslaí was informed by the Chief of Staff via the Military Secretary that his suggestion for a War Records office 'could not be entertained,' owing to the policy of the National Army at that time of abolishing some of the corps and branches created as wartime measures and reducing the strength of the Army in general. Béaslaí rejected this proposition, informing the Chief of Staff that this would not constitute the creation of a new department, but serve to regulate work already being done.[6] Despite his protestations, Béaslaí was told that in the current circumstances his suggestion could 'scarcely be urged,'[7] and in August, Captain Burke was detailed to return to his previous appointment. This doubly stung Béaslaí, as not only did he believe that it rendered Burke's work up until that date useless, 'but the department to which he was recalled – Publicity – was at the time practically non-existent.'[8]

The relationship between Béaslaí and the government on the matter of the Collins biography continued to sour. In September 1924, the President of the Executive Council of Dáil Éireann, W.T. Cosgrave, intimated to Béaslaí (by then a civilian) that he was considering the advisability of relieving him altogether of the work upon which he was engaged. This was considered so sensitive a project that it was deemed necessary to have the matter brought before the Executive Council. Diarmuid O'Hegarty (Secretary to the Executive Council and one time Director of Army Intelligence) expressed concerns regarding sensitive documents to which Béaslaí had access following his departure from the Army.[9]

This episode is illustrative of the fact that control of the 'official narrative' was a significant concern among those responsible for the creation of the new state and foreshadowed the attitude of official Ireland to state records for decades to come. Béaslaí was of the opinion that those who had initially commissioned him to write Collins' biography were doing so in order to exploit Collins' memory in the interests of the Free State. He remarked that 'there were those who wished me to produce a work evolved in hot haste, amid the bitter passions aroused by the Treaty controversy and the Civil War.'[10] It was only after resigning from Dáil Éireann (1923) and the Army (1924) that he felt 'free from official censorship'[11] and in a position to put pen to paper. As will be discussed later, Béaslaí's work also raised the hackles of some on the anti-Treaty side who were equally concerned with controlling the narrative of revolutionary Ireland, with his house being raided by members of the IRA looking to take possession of documents which they considered detrimental to their cause.

Upon his retirement from the Army in August 1924, holding the rank of Major General (having eventually been gazetted as such, rectifying his previous ignominy), Béaslaí was awarded the respectable Military Service Pension of £350 per year. Still a young man, even after contributing so much to the struggle for independence, he returned to writing. In 1926 he finally published the two-volume *Michael Collins and the Making of a New Ireland,* followed by *Michael Collins: Soldier and Statesman* in 1937. His biography only gets more topical, as primary sources, scholarship, and the distance of time increase, being contemporarily lauded and lambasted in terms ranging from the closest to Collins' life both emotionally and chronologically,[12] to hagiographical.[13]

While Béaslaí's own archival ambitions for the new Army had come to naught, the story of the Military Archives was just beginning.

Chapter 1

1924–1926: THE MILITARY
ARCHIVES ESTABLISHED

While Béaslaí's request to the Chief of Staff for the establishment of a 'War Records' department was unsuccessful, there still existed a definite requirement for such a facility within the Army. This began to evolve during February of 1924 when the Director of Intelligence, Colonel Michael Joseph 'MJ' Costello, wrote to the Chief of Staff about the organisation of his Intelligence Branch Staff. Among the many areas covered in this letter, Costello raised the pressing necessity of 'the investigation of…persons claiming under the Army Pensions Bill in respect to people killed during the period 1916 to 1921' and recommending that the 'responsibility for the investigation of these and other matters, usually referred to Intelligence for inquiries, should be fixed.' The establishment of the Intelligence Branch at that time included the appointment of *Officer-in-Charge of Records,* who had a role in verifying particulars of service for the purposes of the recently introduced Army Pensions Act 1923 and Military Service Pensions Act 1924. More of these Acts and amendments would follow, nearly a century later becoming the basis of the *Military Service (1916-1923) Pensions Collection,* the foremost archival collection documenting the Irish revolutionary period.

In April of the same year, Costello wrote again to the Chief of Staff, this time with specifics, requesting an increase in the established strength of the Intelligence Branch in order to enable it to have at least fifteen

1

sergeant clerks. Of a strength of one colonel, three commandants, six captains, three lieutenants, ten NCOs, four privates and fourteen civilians, Costello informed the Chief of Staff that routine work, which included working with records, was absorbing the entirety of that staff with the exception of two captains and four privates. Costello's recommendation was for the Intelligence Branch to be increased by one major, three more commandants, three more captains, one more lieutenant and no less than *forty* sergeant or civilian clerks.[1]

In December, Costello wrote a letter to the Chief of Staff entitled 'Historical Documents and the Formation of Military Archives.' In this letter, he informed the Chief of Staff that the Press Survey Section of Army Intelligence had, for some time, been collecting information for the compilation of what were described as 'war diaries, historical calendars etc' – a sort of chronological historical treatment of the revolutionary and Civil War periods. In the course of this work Costello's staff had 'recently discovered a quantity of very valuable documents, most of which have reached the historical stage.'[2]

These records were, at that time, under the charge of a Thomas Galvin, who had joined the Army as a civilian clerk in the Operations Branch, a sub-branch of the Chief of Staff's Branch, shortly after the Civil War, but was very soon attached to the Intelligence Branch at their request.[3] Galvin's duties included maintaining a newspaper archive and dealing with internal requests for historical data, particularly in support of claims made under the 1924 Military Service Pensions Act. This important function of the early Military Archives must not be overlooked or underestimated as a motivation for its establishment. In the run up to the Army Crisis, the Army had grown bloated from Civil War necessity but still reflected the territoriality of the War of Independence IRA structure. By 1924 it had developed into several powerful fiefdoms with many hardened fighting men who harboured resentment at the severe and rapid demobilisation that followed the Civil War. Colonel Charles Russell's description evokes the period vividly, in which he recalled to the Army Inquiry Committee that:

The GOCs [General Officers Commanding] were most powerful men. They lived in castles all over the country, each with his little Army, and when they came to Dublin to attend meetings, they brought with them in their minds their armies, and backed up their arguments with the power of their positions.[4]

The Military Service Pensions Act of 1924 was an invaluable tool in taking the sting out of the post-Civil War deconstruction of these fiefdoms, particularly against the backdrop of the Army Mutiny as the first serious challenge to the fledgling Free State and the authority of its government.

The documents under Galvin's charge at that time included old records from the Royal Hospital Kilmainham that had belonged to the British administration and comprised the 'Correspondence and Papers of the Commanders-in-Chief of the Forces in Ireland 1784–1894,' also known simply as the 'Kilmainham Papers.' These records were discovered discarded in a cellar in the main building of Army GHQ, removed to the office in Room 40 and placed under Galvin's charge.

Costello also identified the fact that the British 'War Office' in Dublin Castle was still practically intact and contained a quantity of similarly valuable documents. He was especially keen that these records be taken over immediately, noting that the 'War Office' was never formally handed over to any department of the Free State Government and was under the temporary care of Thomas Markham. Markham had previously been placed in Dublin Castle by Michael Collins to act as a conduit between himself and the British Government, and his eccentricities would mean that, for a period after Collins' death, he became a thorn in the side of the new administration.

The second quantity of material under the care of Galvin at that time was made up of approximately 7,000 intelligence records from the Civil War period. These broadly consisted of files, reports and newspaper cuttings. They referred to a range of subjects including the National Army, the Irregular Forces and their activities, the IRA Organisation (IRAO),

Labour and Communist activities and Irish organisations abroad, as well as operational reports.

The *Kilmainham Papers* and the *Civil War Intelligence and Operations Records* constituted the initial holdings of the early Military Archives. Recognising their significance and keen to maintain momentum, Costello recommended that:

> A proper Military Historical Section should be set up into which would be gathered all material of historical value, including those papers at present in the custody of Mr Galvin, the 'War Office' at the Castle, and various material relating to the Republican Army, its organisation and activities since 1916, which material is at present in the hands of various officers and civilians throughout the country. Such a Historical Section would be of very great value and would provide a happy hunting ground for editors of our Military Journal and for those of our officers with a leaning for research work.[5]

On 20 December 1924, Colonel Seamus Woods, the Military Secretary, provided his recommendations to the Chief of Staff that:

> The Director of Intelligence's suggestion is a good one and with the material at our disposal it can easily be put into practice forthwith. The necessity for such a section as he refers to in para 3 of his letter has already arisen and is occupying the GSO 1 Staff Duties attention at the moment: the Secretary Military Service Pensions has asked for the names of officers who served on GHQ Staff or the Army Council since 1916 and it just happens that Major Ryan can practically recall these from memory but in one particular case a doubt has arisen.
>
> For the present this work could be done by the Press Survey Section of Intelligence Branch and the Officer-in-Charge (Commandant Whitmore) is I suggest most suitable for it. Colonel O'Connor is anxious that Mr Galvin should be transferred to Intelligence Branch and, with your sanction, this can be arranged.

As regards the 'War Office' in the Castle I respectfully suggest that you discuss this matter personally with the minister and if possible have the material transferred over without ceremony or prolonged communications on the matter.

The Chief of Staff proceeded to approve the establishment of a Military Archives under the control of Captain Alphonsus Blake. He was assisted by Thomas Galvin, who was subsequently transferred from Operations to Intelligence in order to regularise his appointment.

CAPTAIN 'FONSE' BLAKE

Alphonsus Joseph 'Fonse' Blake came from Thomond Gate, County Limerick. He was a close personal friend of Seán McDermott and extremely active in both the Volunteer and Sinn Féin movements. Blake had been a member of the old Cumann na nGaedhael (Limerick Young Ireland Society), of the first National Council of Sinn Féin, and of the first Committee of Sinn Féin in Limerick. He had been Treasurer of the Wolfe Tone Club in Limerick and one of the founders of the Irish Volunteers in that county, remaining a member of the Volunteers / IRA from November 1913 until February 1922.

Blake was dismissed from employment in the Limerick Labour Exchange in 1919 for refusing to undertake to sever his connection to the Volunteers and Sinn Féin, enduring a year of unemployment as a result. In 1920, Blake was the Joint Secretary of the Limerick Sinn Féin Executive and in 1922, at the request of Major General Fionan Lynch (later Minster for Fisheries) he left well-paying employment as the secretary of a health insurance and a land and labour society to help the Army. In this, he acted in the capacity of Field Censor and Publicity Agent (editor of War News) under Lynch.

Blake came into the Army proper on 7 February 1923. Initially serving as Limerick Command Intelligence Officer, by 1924 he was based in the Intelligence Branch, GHQ. He was described by Major General Michael

Brennan (later Chief of Staff) as 'one of the most capable, conscientious, and hardworking officers in the Army.'[6] There is a sad irony to this, given the circumstances of his retirement from the Army in 1926, as will be described further in this chapter.

THE MILITARY ARCHIVES: DRAFT OF PROPOSED ESTABLISHMENT[7]

On 5 January 1925 the Kilmainham Papers were transferred from Operations Branch to the Archives and, along with intelligence files, reports and surveys, records of the Military Reports and Statistics Department, Command Reports and newspaper cuttings, formed the entirety of the new Military Archives' holdings. This was, however, something of an *ad hoc* arrangement. The accommodation provided for these important records was still entirely unsuited to anything of an ambitious nature and remained to be addressed.

On 11 February 1925, Colonel Costello directed Thomas Galvin to draft a proposed formal establishment for a Military Archives and one week later Galvin presented it to him. In this document, Galvin identified seven objectives for the Military Archives: the custody of military state papers; filing, indexing and cataloguing; preserving the records of the service; military research; relieving departments of surplus files; reception of papers contributed from private sources; and précis work. Galvin's report is an interesting and important document in the early development of the Military Archives. Whether through experience or intuition, Galvin's proposals demonstrated an acute awareness of considerations that remain relevant to the archival profession to the present day.

THE MILITARY ARCHIVES: OBJECTIVES

The first of Galvin's stated objectives, 'the custody of military state papers,' foreshadowed by many decades the Military Archives being designated a statutory 'place of deposit' under the National Archives of Ireland Act, 1986, proposing that 'the Archives would form a Military section of the National Archives, and would be secret. They would be attached to the Minister for Defence, with powers delegated by the President in whom all State papers are vested by law.'

The inclusion of the clause of secrecy mentioned here is worth expanding upon. Irish policy of access to state records from independence until the 1970s has been described as one of a combination of rigid control over access and wilful neglect, in an attempt to 'confine the interpretation of the past, particularly the recent past, to the perception advanced by the republican revolutionary generation.'[8] Béaslaí was even starker in his description at that time, that 'many people seemed anxious to forget the brave and brilliant achievements of the years 1916–1921.'[9] The Military Archives was not developing in a vacuum. In many aspects it reflected the conservativism and attitudes of its place and time. It was not envisioned as the objective agent of citizen advocacy and state accountability in the way that modern national archives are understood. That said, it was a very progressive project relative to the standards of the time.

In relation to the second objective, 'filing,' Galvin identified the importance of proper filing and cataloguing techniques as the efficiency of the work done would 'depend largely on the facility of researching the information available' and proposed to file by department, branch and subject. While this may seem like a statement of the obvious, it is both a mark of the professional operation envisioned by Galvin, in contrast to the reportedly sub-standard practices being employed at that time by Thomas Markham at the State Papers Office in Dublin Castle.

In his third stated objective, Galvin recognised the value of 'records of the service to military heritage' commenting that 'every nation guards with the utmost care the history of its fight for freedom' and that one of the roles of the Military Archives would be 'to perpetuate the memory of those who gave their services on the field, or in any engagement, and to collect any information bearing on the past military battles fought on our soil.' While a relatively progressive proposal in and of itself within the Army, the Military Archives would give primacy to the preservation of the lineage and heritage of the victorious side of the Civil War, with the records of the actions of the anti-Treaty forces and commanders serving as educational resources – tactical and strategic case studies for the military training of the commanders and staff officers of the regular forces.

On the objective of the Military Archives in supporting 'military research,' while this was again to the immediately practical purpose of staff studies and the lessons of war and military organisation, Galvin suggested that pre-Truce British records in particular 'might be opened to historical writers, regimental historians and archivists.' Again, while indicating the value of preserving records from more than one source, the implied access methodology is cautious and prescriptive. Again, this is not a criticism per se but an important observation in understanding both Galvin's motivations and his environment.

In his consideration of a role for the Military Archives in 'relieving departments of surplus files,' Galvin was clearly cognisant of an already existing significant accumulation of files in several Army branches. Galvin noted that many of these records would be valuable for future study and that a formal Military Archives was 'necessary to make provisions for the future.' The importance of appraisal by archivists to identify which records only have current (primary) value and which have informational or evidential future (secondary) value, due to the sheer volume of records generated by modern bureaucracies, was only popularised amongst the archival profession three decades later by the American archivist Theodore Schellenberg.

Galvin put significant value on 'papers contributed from private sources,' his sixth identified objective for the Military Archives, in faithfully documenting the pre-1922 period in particular. In his recommendation on the scope and content of the private collections that should be sought out, Galvin said that,

These include the whole of the Volunteer period, which must be reconstructed from private sources. They also include all pre-22 documents. There are numerous collections and papers stored, buried, locked up and put away in Dublin and other parts of the country. I am already promised some of the collections. Without the establishment of the Military Archives on a public footing it is obviously impossible to secure these valuable memorials, which are all the more important on account of the light they throw on the early stages of our military organisation and its remarkable growth.

Finally, on the objective of the Military Archives in preparing 'précis work,' Galvin was again aware of the potential role for the archive in supporting and informing decision making as well as accountability and advocacy, even if this was limited to officialdom.

There will be queries coming from the Government, the Oireachtas, Army and other sources. There will be questions to be answered, datas to be supplied, chronologies to be prepared, diaries to be written up, calendars to be extracted, reports on various periods to be issued, papers to be edited, documents to be authenticated, accounts of captured papers to be rendered, and the work generally thrown into narrative form, so that the records can be made readily understood and their results analysed. For this purpose, precis will have to be made and the extracts edited.

THE MILITARY ARCHIVES: SOURCES

Galvin's report identified seven potential sources of material for the Military Archives: The 'Kilmainham Papers' (as mentioned already, they were in Galvin's custody at the time of his writing the report), the 'Castle Papers,' the 'GHQ Papers,' the 'Portobello Papers,' the 'Merrion Papers,' the 'Libraries Papers' and 'Private Collections.' His descriptions give a vivid insight into the kind of establishment envisioned.

The 'Kilmainham Papers,' also known as the 'Royal Hospital Papers,' were the British military records covering what Galvin described as the 'British Defence of Ireland' going back to the establishment of the Royal Hospital in 1684. These, along with the Commander-in-Chiefs' correspondence running from 1784 to 1894 and some later papers, constituted the collection. Galvin estimated that the entire collection could have been rendered available for staff research work in about a year, as the papers were already collected and indexed in eighteen sections comprised of approximately 500 volumes. Furthermore, Galvin proposed rapidly extending the work by allotting it to volunteer researchers in connection with the (envisioned, but yet to be established) Military College.

The 'Castle Papers' were those Military Papers at Dublin Castle previously mentioned as being under the custody of Thomas Markham which, at the time of Galvin's report, had not yet been examined except in so far as they had been extracted and published in the Calendar of State Papers. Galvin had the foresight to see the value of holding these papers in connection to the 'Kilmainham Papers,' noting that 'the Royal Hospital Papers largely consist of the correspondence of the Commander in Chief with the Castle. The replies or corresponding communications ought to lie in Castle.' That said, between the signing of the Anglo-Irish Treaty on 6 December 1921 and the handover of the Castle on 16 January 1922, the staff at Dublin Castle had been busy identifying records for burning and those for immediate removal back to Britain. In fact, this probably went on right up until the formal transfer of functions from British to Irish Free State officials in April of that year. So, while of high evidential value to the new state, the 'Castle Papers' could in no way be considered to be complete. For Under-Secretary John Anderson and his staff at the Castle, the transfer of public records was a delicate one. Handover en masse 'would have been to put at risk...reputations, employment and even...lives.'[10]

Thomas Markham was one of Michael Collins' trusted spies in Dublin Castle during the War of Independence. By the time that the Provisional Government took over Dublin Castle, Markham had been appointed by Collins to a position vaguely entitled 'Civil Officer-in-Charge.' The offices he occupied contained the Papers in question, and it was reported that 'he had not a very pleasant position because certain people, described as British Agents, were endeavouring to obtain possession of a portion of the papers under his charge.'[11] Markham, by all accounts, was a considerably eccentric character who had developed grossly exaggerated notions of his role, claiming that Collins had entrusted him with the custody of *all* state papers.[12] With Collins' death, Markham's claims about the precise scope and depth of the responsibilities entrusted to him became impossible to categorically confirm or refute. By 1924, Markham had become an active hindrance to government efficiency and the decision was made that he had to be removed from the Castle.

An increasingly unstable Markham dug in his heels and was evidently becoming a threat to the safety of the records and the reputation of the fledgling Government. It was not until early 1925, the same year that Galvin wrote his 'Draft Establishment,' that the eagerly sought 'Castle Papers' were removed from Markham's care and ended up in the custody of the Ministry of Finance in a rather dramatic episode. While a reorganisation of the Civil Service was taking place, the Establishment Officer at Government Buildings took the opportunity to transfer Markham to a new post. Markham, however, decided that the Government did not have the authority to sanction his transfer and in the end officials from the Ministry of Finance, accompanied by officials from the Board of Works, had to force entry, occupy the offices and change the locks.[13]

The papers that interested Galvin were specifically 'the Military Papers in the Castle' dating back to the time of Queen Elizabeth. In his memo, Galvin explained that there had been an Irish War Office, sometimes called the Military Department, in Dublin Castle. This department oversaw the Irish Military Establishment, which was separate from the British, at least until the Act of Union.

Galvin's analysis of the 'GHQ Papers' is the most noteworthy for several reasons. Firstly, it contributes to the evidence that its founders wanted to create an archive that was not just an adjunct to or surrogate for the previous Directorate of Publicity, but a faithful repository of documentary evidence in the national (i.e., Free State) interest. Secondly, it demonstrates an understanding of the benefit of the Military Archives as a strategic asset that would facilitate decision making and war gaming through the study of real-life courses of action:

> The Papers at GHQ consist of the Departmental correspondence and other documents. The collection of Captured Documents and the personal files built up by Intelligence alone constitute a complete Archives of the Irregulars. The collection of files in this branch is unique in quantity and quality. The documents of the 1922–23 period are exceedingly valuable for the study of organisation and tactics designed to secure internal tranquillity and to meet the problems which arose during the disturbances of that violent period. Here too can be studied at first hand the ideas of Lynch, Deasy, O'Malley, and other Guerrilla chiefs. Much can be learned from the manner in which they dealt with the military problems and external difficulties they encountered.
>
> An analysis of the result of the various moves and counter moves during the 5 or 6 years of guerrilla warfare would make it possible to arrive at important conclusions. It would show the effect on the opponents of various countermoves, and would prove the methods which have been most effective in reaching the desired objectives. It would be possible to say which methods brought in the most results.
>
> These files which would require to be analysed number at present some forty-thousand. Many of them represent heavy dossiers built up from many sources containing very numerous and varied papers, which contain the unfettered expressions of opinion of leaders, giving the secret history of transactions which could not be divulged at the moment, but which will be of great historical importance later on.

Galvin's description of these records, particularly the reference to 'the secret history of transactions which could not be divulged at the moment' is especially thought-provoking in the light of the 'Burn Order' which was to come seven years later, issued by Desmond FitzGerald of Cumann na nGaedheal in anticipation of the handover of power to Fianna Fáil, ordering the destruction of sensitive files from the Civil War period including Intelligence Reports.

The 'Libraries Papers' referred to the military state papers in the custody of the National Library and Trinity College Library. Galvin advocated their cataloguing and the production of précis for the Military Archives, enabling them to be used without taking them away from their custodians. Galvin also identified relevant Irish military papers in the British Museum and Paris Archives, and proposed similar treatment.

In relation to the 'Portobello Papers' and the 'Merrion Street Papers,' Galvin's report simply notes 'papers not examined.' Presumably the 'Portobello Papers' were the records of Army GHQ while based at Portobello Barracks during the Civil War, and Merrion Street Papers referred to the fact that Merrion Square was the home of the Provisional Government's Departmental Headquarters during the War of Independence.

This left 'Private Collections' as the final potential resource in his report. It was from these that Galvin proposed that the Irish Volunteer section of the Military Archives would be built up. Galvin's analysis of this is revealing and prescient for two reasons. Firstly, it foreshadowed the efforts of the Military Archives in the 1930s to collect testimony on the revolutionary period, with varying but generally lower-than-expected levels of success, until the establishment of the Bureau of Military History in the 1940s. Secondly, he very clearly anticipated the future value of the Military Service Pension files, which now constitute the most valuable source of archival evidence on the revolutionary period. Galvin wrote that:

It is from these that the Volunteer Section must be built up. I have already constructed a Roll of the First Volunteer Convention, and from this I think it would be possible on the snowball principle to obtain officers lists of the early Corps, Companies and Battalion formations and Brigade areas. This period is important for the study of territorial organisation. An analysis of the results obtained would provide important data. Much information could be obtained from The Irish Volunteer, but copies of that official organ are exceedingly scarce and I have not been able to trace a single complete file of all the bound volumes of An tÓglách. Indeed, the story of this publication would require a history in itself. I think it is important that the Military Archives of our country should possess a complete file of it in all its forms. Many of the articles written deal with matters of great interest and practical military importance.

The Military Pensions Committee is at present engaged on information as regards claims. In the course of time much information will be available from this source for the Archives. It is possible however that the work of the latter could be organised so as to provide certain data for checking claims.

The most important private collections are in the hands of those appointed to organise the Army when it came under An Dáil. These collections contain the early history of our own military organisation. But I understand they are private property and cannot be brought in under regulations. The establishment of Military Archives appears to provide an opportunity to accept as a public trust any papers of this period which the holders may desire to deposit for the benefit of the Nation.

Some of the prominent individuals identified by Galvin and Blake as possessing papers of interest included General Richard Mulcahy (IRA papers), Major General Seán Mac Mahon (copy of evidence giving history of National Army) and Bulmer Hobson (Volunteer records).

THE MILITARY ARCHIVES: STAFFING AND ORGANISATION

Regarding the organisation of the Military Archives, Galvin proposed that it be placed as part of the official establishment of the Intelligence

Branch. He believed that this was the best place within the Army establishment as it would serve to protect the Military Archives in the most complete manner. It would safeguard, he proposed, against theft, spies, secret service agents and would ensure safety, security and secrecy. The Intelligence Branch's system of receiving and circulating intelligence he considered as the most useful and the one which would guarantee accessions of suitable materials.

Under Galvin's proposal, the Officer-in-Charge of the Archives would report directly to the Director of Intelligence, ensuring supervision and efficiency under military control. Galvin's report again proved itself to be prescient as it recommended that the President of the Executive Council empower the Minister for Defence to form the Military Archives and to have deposited there the existing state papers – again anticipating the future designation of the Military Archives as a 'place of deposit' under the National Archives of Ireland Act.

Galvin's description of the proposed accommodation for the Military Archives also demonstrated a firm understanding of the practical considerations involved with operating an archival reading room and repository:

> Situation of Archives inside in barracks is safest and best. This would save the cost of a guard. Two passes would be required, one to enter the barracks, the second a special pass to the Archives...A strong room would be constructed or adapted and documents deposited in tin boxes...A long room would be required for filing and cataloguing, and small rooms for research work and precis.

Finally, in relation to the staffing of the Military Archives, Galvin was no less familiar with the necessary professional requirements.

> The first appointment would be that of a person to examine and take over collections. This would enable him to work with a small staff, which could be regulated to deal with the accessions and would prevent the swamping

of the Archives in the early years. When the preliminary collections were made the post of Examiner would merge into that of Archivist, that is to say the nature of the work would change from collections to literary direction. [In order to simplify matters, the following day Galvin submitted an amendment, removing the suggestion of appointing an Examiner and replacing it with the immediate appointment of an Archivist]. The archivist would have in fact the primary duty of examining all papers. He would be assisted by persons to register, number and index documents, to file and catalogue them. The Catalogues would be made out by taking each number on the Index, entering particulars of the matters dealt with, extended to show subjects and actions taken. From the Catalogues the card index of subjects could be built. These operations would require a Staff consisting of a filist, cataloguist and card indexer; in addition to the Archivist who would lay out the work simultaneously and progressively.

It is suggested that the post of Military Archivist might be an established Civil Post attached to the Ministry of Defence with a status corresponding to the nature and responsibilities of his office, which would be confidential and delicate. He would be in charge of the Archives reporting to the Director of Intelligence.

He would work under the general supervision of the Officer-in-Charge of State Papers and would keep that officer in touch with the Military Section by rendering periodical returns to show the materials collected and the progress of the work, and would furnish to him any available data required by Government. He would conform with the general regulations governing Public Archives, which would be issued by the President through the Officer-in-Charge State Papers.

Colonel Costello consulted his Staff Officer, Commandant William James Brennan-Whitmore, for advice and observations. Brennan-Whitmore was impressed, describing the scheme in general as 'excellent.' However, he did express concerns in relation to Galvin's proposal for a civilian to be in charge of the Military Archives. This was based primarily on the fact that the military authority over such a person would be very limited, and should that person be raised to Civil Service status their power over him would be reduced to nearly nil. Also, the authority of a civilian over military subordinates, he suggested, could very easily be non-existent in practice. Brennan-Whitmore further expressed concern about the potential dangers of civil service and political interference in colourful terms.

> There is a danger of putting up such a scheme as complete as this prematurely. Suppose that when the scheme (with Civil Service control and a good salary) comes before the Executive Council, and one of the members have a pullet that never laid any eggs but is quite willing to hatch on a snug nest, and suppose that pullet is nominated over Galvin's head, what then? Are we to have two civilian archivists? For this reason, I avoided putting up a complete scheme in my letter of agitation on this subject.[14]

While the parameters and limits of control remain a live and contentious issue to this day between the Defence Forces and the Department of Defence, it is important to bear in mind that these events took place in the shadow of the Army Mutiny and the publication of the report of the Army Inquiry Committee less than a year previously. A degree of suspicion, or at least tentativeness, is unsurprising.

Taking Brennan-Whitmore's advice into consideration, Costello forwarded the report to the Chief of Staff the following week. In his covering letter Costello emphatically advised that no such plan could be initiated without first addressing the issue of suitable accommodation (it would not be the last time), the situation at that time being deemed as categorically unsuitable.

FORMAL ESTABLISHMENT PROPOSED TO THE MINISTER FOR DEFENCE

On 30 March 1925, the Chief of Staff, Lieutenant General Peadar MacMahon, forwarded the proposal to establish the Military Archives on a formal footing to the Minister for Defence. MacMahon's proposal

expanded on Galvin's draft report in its insistence on the importance of
the project:

> I do not think it necessary to enlarge upon the main heads under which
> the necessity for a Military Archives is set out, beyond stating that these
> documents are definitely the property of the State, as the records of titles
> and the deeds to real estate property; or as the records of the Acts of the
> Peoples Parliament set upon the Statute Book of the State. As military
> documents they are peculiar to our charge, and it behoves us to guard
> them with jealous care and solicitude as part Trustees for the State.[15]

In the meantime, conditions on the ground remained sub-standard. In
April 1925, the Director of Intelligence had the documents and books that
formed the nucleus of the Military Archives moved from their location
in Room 40 at GQH, Parkgate, to the nearby Red House on Infirmary
Road. This direction was given as a temporary arrangement only, as the
Red House accommodation was deemed unsuitable, but was an interim
measure while Costello formally requested permanent accommodation
for the Military Archives in a building in McKee Barracks, Blackhorse
Avenue, known as the 'Recreation Establishment.'[16]

By June of 1925, the Chief of Staff had still received no reply from the
Minister for Defence and on the third of that month wrote again. The
Chief of Staff reminded the Minister that the matter had been pending
since the previous November and requested that it have his immediate attention. Most pressingly, MacMahon sought clarification on the
immediate need for a decision on the sanction for the proposed scheme,
the allocation of a suitable building and any necessary structural alter-
ation, and the authority to take in all files and documents of military
importance which were at present in the Royal Hospital Kilmainham,
Dublin Castle and Government Buildings.[17]

By November 1925, the Minister had still made no reply to the Chief
of Staff. On 16 November the Chief of Staff wrote yet again to the
Minster, advising him that since his previous letters he had located a

suitable building for the housing of the Military Archives, namely, the Library in the Hibernian Military School in the Phoenix Park. The Chief of Staff described the site as a suitable building standing by itself, made even more suitable by the fact that the Hibernian School was, at that time, earmarked to become the Military College. The Military Archives, he argued, could be co-located with the War Museum, which was also anticipated for the site. While none of this came to pass it demonstrates MacMahon's clear ambition for military heritage. In this same letter, MacMahon again reminded the Minister that even if a decision had not been made on the 'Castle Papers,' by then wrested from Markham's zealous custodianship into that of the Ministry for Finance, that if permission could be granted to take up the premises in the Phoenix Park that they could begin work with the material currently at their disposal.[18]

MacMahon's proactive approach still received no reply from the Minister, and the following week he had the Assistant Chief of Staff, Major General Aodh MacNeill, write yet again to the Minister's office on the matter. Two days later the following non-committal reply arrived via C.B. O'Connor, the Secretary to the Department of Defence and First World War veteran:

> The Minister duly saw the Chief of Staff's letter and decided to put it aside for a time until he found the opportunity to give it the careful consideration which the proposal involved requires. I shall put the matter on the Agenda for a meeting of the Council of Defence which will probably be held next week.[19]

The next meeting of the Council of Defence was held on 14 December 1925, with the Minister and Chief of Staff both in attendance. While the topic of 'Works to be undertaken by Board of Works in 1926-1927' was included on the agenda, and the matter of suitable accommodation for the Army Finance Office in the precincts of Headquarters at Parkgate was discussed, the Military Archives was not.[20]

It can be argued that the Minister's reticence may have been indicative of a reluctance by government to formally establish a Military Archives.

In a memorandum written five years later, in 1930, Captain Niall Charles Harrington would note that:

> This matter [the Castle Papers] and the question of the Minister's approval of the establishment of Archives was referred to the Minister for Defence, Mr Peter Hughes, who deferred his decision until he could examine the whole question thoroughly. No further action appears to have been taken.[21]

On the other hand, it is important to examine these events within the broader considerations of the time and not just in isolation. To do this it is necessary to understand something of the Army and the Department of Defence – two organisations not as separately demarked in 1924 as they are now – as they existed and operated at that time. The Civil War had only ended in 1923 and the Army Inquiry Committee, tasked with investigating the circumstances surrounding the Army Mutiny of early 1924, had only completed its work and presented its findings to the Executive Council during the summer of that same year. The Army and the Department of Defence were still in a formative phase. During 1925, for example, the Council of Defence was having memoranda prepared for its consideration on the organisation of the United States War Department, Command of the Forces and Duties and Heads of Branches, with a view to finalising its own organisation – and of course preparing the groundwork for the Military Mission to the USA in 1926 which would have a very significant effect on the structure and establishment of the Defence Forces. In fact, the country had no formal defence policy at all at the time and would not, until the Army Organisation Board of 1926 completed its work and presented its findings. It could be theorised that the Cumann na nGaedheal government was reluctant to dig up the skeletons of the recent past, but it could also be theorised that it simply had other, more pressing concerns.

As an example of the sort of organisation and arrangement that was going on at that time, the Commissioner of Public Works wrote to the Secretary of the Department of Defence on 25 July 1925 expressing his:

...difficulty in considering any proposals for new works at Military Barracks until we are in possession of an authorised programme for the permanent distribution of the Army. We are told that it is desired to concentrate the troops in a comparatively small number of stations, which they will occupy in sufficient numbers to make efficient training practicable, but no indication of where, or how, this concentration is to be effected has reached us.[22]

Well into 1926 the Department of Finance was directing that the Royal Hospital Kilmainham be examined by a delegation led by the Quartermaster General in order to see whether it would be suitable to accommodate the entire Department of Defence with a view to discussing the matter with the Commissioners of Public Works.[23] A considerable portion of Council of Defence meetings during 1925 and 1926 was dedicated to trying to figure out where exactly, now that the Free State had this new Defence Forces and associated department of state, they were going to put everybody.

THE ANTI-TREATY ARCHIVE

For students of archivistics, the Military Archives is an excellent case study of the development of a state archive from its inception and within a discrete duration. The objectives described in the 1925 'Draft Proposed Establishment,' which aimed to put a formal structure on what had been operating on a more *ad hoc* basis since 1924, remain familiar to the modern archivist. While the Minister for Defence was proving evasive regarding the Chief of Staff's repeated requests for this nationally important archive to be established formally and officially, during 1925 the anti-Treatyites of Sinn Féin, under Éamon de Valera, were busy trying to establish an archive of their own. The efforts of the anti-Treatyites to secure material for their own archives, quite possibly in reaction in part at least, to the Army's efforts, demonstrate the power of archives and their importance to both sides of the Civil War divide for establishing legitimacy and vouchsafing lineage and identity. For this reason, de Valera's motivations are as worthy of examination as those of Béaslaí, Costello, Galvin and Blake.

This subject was one very close to de Valera's heart. In 1924, while imprisoned in Arbour Hill, he had suggested to his secretary, Kathleen O'Connell, that she should assemble a documentary history of the revolutionary period, from the 1916 Easter Rising up until the end of the Civil War. As a token of his conviction de Valera provided O'Connell with a 25-page set of instructions of how and where she could source the necessary information for its compilation,[24] mirroring in some ways what Galvin had produced for Costello. This was an ambition that Dorothy Macardle would eventually fulfil through her book *The Irish Republic*, undertaken at de Valera's request in 1925 and taking 11 years to complete.[25]

More than this, David McCullagh's two-volume, 2017 biography of de Valera suggests a man deeply concerned with controlling narratives and perceptions; something towards which he was naturally orientated and at which he was adept as someone who inspired a cult of personality - a personality that had 'marked him out for advancement by his superiors in the Volunteers'[26] even though, by all accounts, his military prowess was negligible.

Upon his release from prison in 1924, de Valera had immediately assumed chairmanship of meetings of Cohmairle na dTeachtaí, an alternative parliament made up of anti-Treaty members of the Second Dáil who believed themselves to be the legitimate de jure Republican government through their lineage to that assembly. An alternative parliament, by necessity, requires an alternative claim to legitimacy and accompanying historiography. McCullagh notes that Mary MacSwiney, who had played a key organisational role within Sinn Féin during de Valera's imprisonment and who took over as party leader in 1927, was suspicious of de Valera's tendency towards political revisionism.[27] During 1924 de Valera had begun, for example, to publicly claim that he would never have signed the Anglo-Irish Treaty until the issue of partition was settled, 'a gross distortion of his position in 1921'.[28] De Valera was also obsessed with the press and unsuccessfully attempted to attain the defunct *Freeman's Journal*. He would go on to fulfil this ambition through the establishment of the *Irish Press* in 1931. Even when he founded Fianna Fáil in 1926 it was a name chosen to deliberately imply a lineage back to the Irish Volunteers and more, 'representing a tradition that went back much further than its own establishment.'[29]

In October 1925 a raid took place on the home of Piaras Béaslaí, at that point retired from the Army and working on his biography of Michael Collins. The report of the Eastern Command Intelligence Officer noted that the raid was carried out 'at the instrumentality of [Michael] Chadwicke, 6th Battalion (Irregulars)'[30] and that it had been carried out by men from Dun Laoghaire, among which Eugene Davis was named specifically. Both Chadwick and Davis were well known anti-Treaty IRA commanders in that area. The raid was carried out as it was believed that Béaslaí had in his possession many documents to be used in the publishing of his book that would have been damaging to the anti-Treaty cause.

On 5 October 1925, Commandant Brennan-Whitmore wrote to Colonel Costello a letter with an attached account from Thomas Galvin, suggesting that the anti-Treaty forces were attempting to establish an archive for their own purposes. These two hand-written documents give an important insight into both sides' understanding of the power of the archive as a tool of bureaucratic evidence, hegemonic expression, legitimacy and authority.

Sir,

Reference attached. This was first told to me in confidence by Mr Galvin; and I instructed him to put it in writing. I do not know what value you may be inclined to place on it; but I am inclined to place a rather high value on it. It appears that the anti Treatyites are working hard on an 'Archives' from their point of view; whereas we seem to be resting largely on our own.

The 'unimpeachable source' Galvin refers to is Mrs Griffiths. He doesn't know the 'secret channel' beyond the fact that he is a business man.

Yours obediently,

WJBW

Galvin's report read as follows:

A Chara,

I learned yesterday from an unimpeachable source that Mr de Valera is making a collection of state papers. He recently approached the 'secret channel' used by the late President Griffith for the transmission of letters to the British Government and endeavoured to obtain from him a full statement of the negotiations and information as to any documents he had in his possession. I am informed that Mr de Valera obtained nothing from this source.

I am informed from the same source that JJ O'Kelly (Scéilg) sits in a room overhead the shop (at Gill's [publishers at 50 Upper O'Connell St, Dublin]) and is there engaged writing what appears to be a record of certain transactions. He has collected a mass of papers and documents. These include the files of the Catholic Bulletin containing his own articles on Easter Week, which I understand he is to publish in book form. He has also a file of 'Nationality.'

I also learned from the same source that when the 'Secret Channel' was in London twelve months ago the then Premier, Mr Ramsey MacDonald [UK Prime Minister 22 January – 4 November 1924], sent for him to Downing Street and there entrusted to him a sealed letter to be delivered to Mr de Valera's own hands. The 'Secret Channel' arrived in Dublin, proceeded to Suffolk Street [Sinn Féin offices] and with great difficulty was admitted to Mr de Valera's room. Mr de Valera was very suspicious and refused at first to take the packet. He sent for Austin Stack, and then they both signed the receipt, which the 'Secret Channel' took back to Mr. Ramsey MacDonald, who quitted office a few weeks later. The receipt was a form provided by him, Ramsey MacDonald, to be taken back to him by the 'Secret Channel.'

Tomás Ó Gealbháin

In his Bureau of Military History Witness Statement given in 1956, JJ O'Kelly (known by the pen name *Scéilg*), who had been a prominent member of the Gaelic League and Deputy Chairman of the first Dáil Éireann in 1919, expressed his own opinion on the status of the material on which he was working, as referred to in Galvin's letter, stating that:

> …there could be no more useful sources of information than the numbers of the Catholic Bulletin from the founding of the Irish Volunteers until the debate on the Articles of Agreement for a Treaty. As editor, I went to the greatest trouble to get details from persons who had themselves taken part in the Rising at the different posts in the city, and I had then carefully checked to ensure that they were correct in every detail, so that the Castle authorities could not accuse us of exaggeration or misrepresentation.[31]

In his statement he also described how 'since long before the Rising, Gills was a clearing house for everybody connected with the national movement.' From all of this it is clear that the Sinn Féin efforts to create its own archive, and thus exercise control over its narrative and public perceptions were no less serious than the Army's – it had the pedigree, the credentials and, where necessary, the ruthlessness to use the IRA to make it happen. This episode illustrates both sides' appreciation of the fundamental role that archives play in establishing and maintaining the legitimacy and lineage of a state.

For professional archivists in particular, the implications are notable. When considering the history and development of the Military Archives in its early days, it is worth doing so through the lens of the archivist Terry Cook's ideas about the shifting archival paradigms of the past century and a half. Cook made the case that during this time

> The archivist has been transformed, accordingly, from passive curator to active appraiser to societal mediator to community facilitator. The focus of archival thinking has moved from evidence to memory to identity and

community, as the broader intellectual currents have changed from pre-modern to modern to postmodern to contemporary.[32]

The records from the formative years of the Military Archives illustrate the transition from the era of the passive curator of juridical legacy to the active appraiser of cultural memory. The most symbolic and dramatic event marking this transition was the destruction of the Public Records Office during the siege of the Four Courts at the outbreak of the Civil War in 1922 – the literal destruction of the institutional embodiment of Cook's first paradigm. The early history of the Military Archives demonstrates a very deliberate and conscious effort to actively collect and commission material documenting the history of the new Army and its role in the foundation of the new state since the foundation of its predecessor organisation, the Irish Volunteers. As Cook described it:

> Seen variously as 'historian-archivists,' or 'handmaidens of historians,' the archivist in this second paradigm discerned appraisal values primarily through the trends in historical writing, and then acquired records as archives to reflect or reinforce those historiographical patterns.[33]

In and of themselves, the motivations of the anti-Treatyites to establish their own archive were no different. Compared, contrasted and contextualised by the efforts of the 'official' side to establish the Military Archives we are presented with a case study of what many prominent archival academics would describe as the role of archives as sources of bureaucratic power and legitimacy, as well as their presentation as contested spaces.[34] It is only in recent decades that the archival profession has changed its perspective away from seeing the archive as 'an institution that systematically promotes, preserves and makes accessible memory, culture and identity in the form of bureaucratic and social evidence'[35] and recognising that it is can be 'contested political space associated with the promotion of asymmetrical power…and the omission or silencing of alternative narratives.'[36]

Nor were de Valera's efforts unusual or unique. Contemporary archival research has shown that the impetus to create *imagined* and *post-hoc* documentation where the state has failed to be a generally applicable one, not just one specific to the case currently under discussion. This is especially so in cases of politicized record-keeping, or where there are discrepancies between official records and the gamut of human experiences typical of Civil War, particularly on the part of the losers or victims.[37] People in such circumstances want their story told, and 'the focus on stories reminds us that much of what is absent from records is filled in social contexts through personal narrative.'[38] Ernie O'Malley and Uinseann Mac Eoin were two prominent individuals who illustrated this point, collecting the personal narratives of many people who took the anti-Treaty side. Through the vehicle of the Bureau of Military History, described by the historian Dr Eve Morrison as 'a cultural initiative of the newly independent state to establish the bona fides of its claim to nationhood' and a 'symbol of republican reconciliation,'[39] the Irish State itself would provide the most significant exemplar of this tendency. In fact, the most important archival sources that exist on the formative years of the modern Irish State – the *Bureau of Military History (1913–1921)* and the *Military Service (1916–1923) Pensions Collection* – consist primarily of *post-hoc* personal testimony.

THOMAS GALVIN'S LEGACY

Thomas Galvin left the Army in 1926, being called to the Bar in November of the following year. He played a key role in the formation of the Military Archives during his brief two-year tenure. The *Memorandum on the General Staff,* which is preserved in the Historical Section papers at the Military Archives, is an example of one of Galvin's undertakings which illustrates the fact that he was engaged on serious intellectual endeavours above what would typically be expected of a general clerk. The motivation behind the *Memorandum* project was very much about giving a historiographical grounding to the new Army; in this case with a focus on the General Staff but the themes of succession and the legitimacy of the new National Army were to be a common thread throughout other projects of the early Military Archives, particularly the *Anglo-Irish Conflict (1913–1921) Project* and the naming of the Volunteer Reserve Regiments in the 1930s.

The aim of Galvin's *Memorandum* was expressed in its opening paragraph, namely, that 'in taking out The Higher Appointments it has been found necessary to trace up the history of the General Staff, so that the succession could be fully determined in the case of each Department and Branch.'[40] The *Memorandum* traced the origin of the General Staff back to the formation of the Sub-Committee of Military Inspection formed in June 1914 by the Provisional Committee of the Irish Volunteers, up to the General Staff as it was constituted at the time of its authoring by Galvin. Again, the utility of this project in establishing the hereditary and legitimacy of the Army's – and by extension, the State's – power, is unambiguous.

Major Ryan, of the Office of the Adjutant General, forwarded Galvin's *Memorandum* to Michael McDunphy for review. McDunphy at that time was the Assistant Secretary to the Executive Council and would go on to be the Director of the Bureau of Military History in the 1940s. With the typical uncompromising attention to detail for which he was known, McDunphy highlighted two particular chronological errors, in relation to periods during which Richard Mulcahy was Minister for Defence 1922–1924, and the timing of Diarmuid O'Hegarty's departure from Army Intelligence and return to the government. He commented that 'there may be other matters which call for revision, but, as I have said, these are items which strike me in the course of casual reading and by no means represent an exhaustive examination. Perhaps you will kindly have the matter looked into.'[41] It is significant to note, not least in light of the refusal of the Minister for Defence to give official sanction for the establishment of the Military Archives despite the repeated petitioning of the Chief of Staff, that the interest in compiling this information extended all the way to the highest levels of Government – so much so that in this case it was personally invigilated, almost to the point of pedantry, by the Assistant Secretary to the Executive Council of Dáil Éireann.

Other projects undertaken by the Military Archives during Galvin's time followed in a similar vein and documented the inauguration, constitution, organisation, strength and executive of the Volunteer Movement. These entailed documenting the names of the members of the Provisional Committee of the Volunteers after the meeting of November 1913. This included those of John Redmond's nominees as accepted by the Provisional Committee in June 1914, the names of the Committee of the Irish Volunteers after the split with Redmond's National Volunteers in October 1914, and the names of the Committee of the Irish Volunteers immediately prior to Easter 1916. This practice of thematic collection continued and was expanded upon during the 1930s under Colonel J.J. 'Ginger' O'Connell.

GALVIN'S DEPARTURE

Thomas Galvin found himself in the midst of a peculiar situation regarding civilian clerks within the Army in late 1925. In a memorandum by the departmental secretary C.B. O'Connor, authored that September for the agenda of the Council of Defence, on the subject of civilian clerks and typists, it was noted that while *Organisation Order No.3* provided only for military clerks, there were, at that time, seventy-one civilian clerks employed throughout the Defence Forces. There was evidently an element of resentment fermenting among certain members of the military towards civilian staff:

> In certain offices objections have been made to the employment of military clerks on the grounds that the work was upset by the absence on parade. It takes a considerable time to train a soldier clerk and frequently as soon as he is trained into the work he is discharged from the Army... The cases of all civilian clerks should be taken up with a view to whether they should be replaced by soldier clerks.[42]

29

In connection to this, the previous week's Council of Defence meeting of 3 September 1925 had recommended a list of civilian clerks for discharge, including the individual employed by Operations Branch of the Chief of Staff's Branch, i.e., Galvin, who had originally been posted to that appointment and subsequently attached to Intelligence. Of the other branches of the Chief of Staff's Branch – Military Secretary, General, Training and Operations, Staff Duties and Intelligence – the only other branch that had civilian clerks was Intelligence, which had 14, none of which were recommended for discharge. The memorandum's recommendation that 'civilian clerks should if necessary be replaced by soldier clerks' would at least give reasonable cause for speculation that there was perhaps more resentment than economy behind it.

The final appearances of Thomas Galvin in the records of the Military Archives surround a peculiar incident. There is no explicit evidence that this incident related to his departure. However, given its general peculiarity and the ill-feeling expressed in the Secretary for Defence's memorandum towards civilian clerks, as well at its proximity to his departure from the Army, it is worth mentioning, if for no other reason than it is a curious anecdote.

On the evening of 7 December 1925, at about 4 p.m., Galvin was engaged in making a précis of a manuscript of government correspondence dating from 1793 when the lights went out throughout the Red House. He went upstairs to see what was wrong. When the lights were restored to the building and he returned to the room in which he was working, the book was missing. Galvin made a verbal report to the duty officer and the following day complied a written report for Captain Blake, which was in turn passed to the Director of Intelligence. The Director queried why Galvin did not make his written report until the following day, to which Galvin responded that he had thought that verbally reporting the matter to the duty officer had been sufficient.[43]

Five months later, by May 1926, Galvin had retired from the Army. A letter to the Minister for Defence from the Assistant Chief of Staff records that 'since writing we have lost the services of Mr Galvin, Civil Servant, who was engaged in looking after the material in our Archives…'[44] With that, Thomas Galvin's brief but impactful relationship with the Military Archives ended.

Compounding the resulting difficulties for the fledgling Military Archives was the loss of Captain Blake around the same time. Having done more than his fair part for his country over the years, Blake resigned his commission in the Army in July 1926, upon his return from an absence resulting from a bout of influenza. Suffering from a congenital disability (Blake had a hare lip and cleft pallet) he was impeded in his ability to carry out any military work other than clerical and felt unsuited to the rigorous officer training courses which were becoming a standard part of Army life as the organisation professionalised. At the age of 42, while he was not old per se, he was old in a young army of young officers, and all of this resulted in his feeling increasingly self-conscious and out of place. While he did not hope to be promoted beyond his current rank, he was finding it increasingly difficult to support his family of seven on a captain's salary.[45]

The loss of Galvin and Blake was disastrous for the fledgling Military Archives. The Chief of Staff petitioned the Executive Council in late-1925 for the loan of Henry Egan Kenny, Librarian to Dublin Castle, for a few months, to assist the Military Archives in its work. The request was never acceded to and further exacerbated the *ad hoc* nature of its work. This left the Chief of Staff in a position where there was 'no suitable man to whom such important work could be entrusted.'[46] As a result, the work of cataloguing, indexing and filing the documents already in the custody of the Military Archives effectively ceased until 1929.

Chapter 2

1926–1932: THE MILITARY ARCHIVES STAGNATES

The latter half of the 1920s was a time of change for the Irish Defence Forces, which officially came into existence under that title on 1 October 1924. This happened under the terms of the Defence Forces (Temporary Provision) Act, 1923 and represented a transition from its previous incarnation as the National Army and the broader Civil War period. In 1926, Colonel M.J. Costello was among a group of officers who travelled as part of the Military Mission to the USA,[1] a significant event in the development of the Defence Forces away from its guerrilla roots and into an increasingly professional force.

The two main objectives of the Military Mission were to make a general study of the United States National Defence Act in operation and of the United States military system, while particularly focusing on their military education. Meanwhile back in Ireland, Costello was replaced by Colonel E.V. O'Carroll, who was appointed as Director of Intelligence on 1 January 1926 and subsequently replaced by Colonel Frederick Henry on 1 August 1927.

Confidential reports from early 1927 to the Chief Staff Officer's (CSO's) Branch record that a reorganisation had taken place within the Army, which saw Intelligence divided into four Sections: A, B, C and D. The corresponding areas of responsibility of these sections were *internal espionage, topographical and statistical, publicity* and *for-*

eign armies respectively.[2] This reorganisation was the result of the work and recommendations of the Army Organisation Board 1925–1926. Following the Civil War, the Army was in a state of flux as it had no stated policy to maintain it. The Board was established in the aftermath of the Army Crisis[3] (1924) by the Chief of Staff, Lieutenant General Peadar MacMahon, in May 1925, in order to examine and report on the necessary modifications in the Defence Forces to enable it to fulfil the functions of a modern army with regard to national defence. As such it was the first major effort to formulate a National Defence Policy on a long-term basis and the report was published by the Department of Defence in July 1926.[4]

For the Intelligence Branch, now known as the Second Bureau, this reorganisation involved the assignment of new duties and responsibilities to its staff.[5] These included responsibility for 'military reference libraries' but the Board's report did not make any reference specifically to archives or other historical work. The confidential reports from the Director of Intelligence to the CSO for 1927 and 1928 chart the progress of the Second Bureau in its new roles and functions.

While Section 'A' was responsible for internal espionage, reports document that 'records' also fell as a sub-section within their remit. In his monthly report to the CSO for January 1927, Colonel O'Carroll noted that 'the ordinary work of this sub-section is being carried out, and is satisfactory. A complete list of all the files in our possession is being completed.'[6] This is the only instance in which work with records is specifically referred to and is not referred to again in any further confidential reports from the Director to the CSO.

The roles and functions of the Second Bureau were reorganised internally during early 1927 due to chronic understaffing. During this time the wider work of Section 'A' also covered the verification of claims made under the Army and Military Service Pensions Acts and spread into what were on paper the functions of other sections of the Bureau. Despite the importance of the Intelligence Branch in supporting claims under the Pensions Acts, there remained a lack of joined-up thinking or wider acknowledgement of the potential benefits of formally establishing the Military Archives. In April of 1927 for example, the Director of Medical Services wrote a memo for the attention of the Council of Defence in view of the passing of the Army Pensions Bill 1927 and the resulting rush of pension claimants, noting the 'absence of any machinery or provision for working this Act.' He suggested the immediate establishment of a Departmental committee, emphasising the necessity that it be chaired by 'a legal man' but with no reference to the use of a functioning archive in supporting its work.[7] The requirements of the Army Pensions Board were growing and this was appreciated. It followed logically that this conferred an increasingly important role on Military Archives in supporting the verification of these claims, but this seems to have been ignored.

This was a time of change and development within the Second Bureau in other ways. The Press Survey sub-section for example cancelled their subscription to several newspapers – many of which were regional including the *Northern Whig*, the *Derry Journal*, the *Dundalk Democrat*, and *Connaught Tribune* – and compiled a new list. This indicated a more outward focus; a change of emphasis from the local and regional to the national and internal subversive threats to the State and consisted of the *Irish Independent, Irish Times, Belfast Telegraph, Morning Post, London Times, An Phoblacht*, the *Irish Statesman*, the *Leader, Honesty* and the *Voice of Labour*.[8]

Despite initially slow progress, by October 1927 the Director was in a position to inform the Chief Staff Officer that:

> The organisation initiated in February last is working very satisfactorily. The officers in charge of the various Sections have a thorough grasp of what is required of them, and are perfecting their technical military knowledge in their own particular sphere.[9]

Things at the Bureau were far from perfect though. One particular problem documented was in relation to the Library, and is worth noting as it was something with which Colonel J.J. O'Connell would also have virtually identical difficulties during his tenure as Officer-in-Charge of the Military Archives from the mid-thirties onward. In this same report the Director described the difficulties in 'procuring books containing data on the technical military subjects dealt with in the Bulletins' (instructional publications produced by the Second Bureau) and how the 'present library consists of books collected in a haphazard way from time to time without regard to the present requirements of the Bureau, and most of the material at our disposal is useless for this purpose.'

The confidential report of 11 January 1928 contains a significant entry headed 'Disposal of Files,' the first reference in this series of reports to records in their own right. Ominously, it notes that the 'files of the Command Intelligence Officer, Cork, had been read over, segregated and transferred to the Garda Síochána,' a reference to the handover of the national intelligence apparatus from the Army to the Garda. From mid-1926 onwards the responsibility for dealing with espionage was transferred from being a military to a policing function. This was a significant transfer of powers and responsibility for the security of the state between the two organisations. The 1924 Army Reports in particular, from General Eoin O'Duffy to the President and Executive Council of Dáil Éireann, demonstrate an extremely powerful intelligence apparatus under his control. During this time O'Duffy held both the appointments of General Officer Commanding the Forces and Commissioner of An Garda Síochána.

The absence of opposition (or at least evidence of opposition) from Henry, as Director of Intelligence, to the transfer of these valuable records from the Army to the Gardaí is interesting in itself, but it is more interesting when compared to the attitude of the successor, Major J.P.M. Cotter. Cotter was an officer with an appreciation of the requirement for the preservation of Army history, advocating for the establishment of a military museum and requesting permission from the Chief of Staff to contact the Director of the National Museum of Ireland with a view to securing any suitable material that may come available as a result of their clearing out of certain exhibits that was going on at the time. Cotter's interest extended to records. In his quarterly report dated 4 January 1929 he challenged the Chief of Staff on the issue of the transfer of intelligence records to the Gardaí, and raised the issue of a military archive, one with a broader scope that simply collecting material relating to the revolutionary period, as it had been up until then. Cotter wrote that:

> I personally have perused and 'dipped into' a great many files in my efforts to make myself au fait with the resources of the Bureau. I am very disturbed indeed to find that machinery which was so effective in 1922–1924 has been handed over to the Civic Guard without the personnel accustomed to using it, and there is reason to believe that the machinery is not now effective...
>
> In my July-September report I mentioned the matter of material for Military Museums. Has anything been done, please? It would be a pity if such valuable material becomes dispersed through inaction. We can certainly store it pending formal authority for Museums and Archives.[10]

In the final paragraph of the following quarterly report, which would be his last as Director of the Second Bureau before being replaced by Colonel J.J. O'Connell, he noted that he was 'still without any instruction or authority in this matter.'[11]

Cotter's tenure at the Second Bureau is significant. While there had been projects like Galvin's *Memorandum on the General Staff* the inaction of the CSO on the matter of 'museums and archives' demonstrates an attitude that runs throughout the story of the Military Archives and was perhaps symptomatic of wider contemporary Irish attitudes to archives previously mentioned. While there was ostensibly an appreciation of the need to document and preserve military history and heritage, this appreciation never managed to go beyond treating it as an ancillary function.

Cotter's clear disapproval of the handover of the Cork Intelligence Officer's files, along with the rest of the Army's intelligence 'machinery' to An Garda Síochána also suggests an understanding of the role of good knowledge management and the subsequent long-term preservation of records as powerful tools in the Army's intelligence arsenal. The current whereabouts of these highly valuable intelligence files, handed over in the mid-1920s, is uncertain. The long-term preservation of records by An Garda Síochána has generally proven inadequate and certainly not on par with their military counterparts. The fact that this was commented upon in the 2007 McEntee Report into the Dublin and Monaghan Bombings of 1974 illustrates the real life implications foreshadowed by Cotter several decades previously.

By the end of 1928 the Military Archives, as it existed, was becoming nobody's child. Heated words were exchanged between Cotter and the Chief Staff Officer, Colonel Seamus O'Higgins. O'Higgins unceremoniously raised with Cotter the matter of 'a room generally described as archives containing the correspondence and books of the British Commander in Chief in Ireland and certain other old papers...' and who should be responsible for their storage. O'Higgins directed Cotter that, since he had recently been provided with a room to store 'presses containing old files of the Second Bureau,' he was to immediately arrange for them to be collected and to have an officer placed in charge of them.

Cotter replied to O'Higgins in even more direct terms. He informed him that no such room had been provided to him, and that old files of the Second Bureau were stored elsewhere. He also pointed out that he personally held the key to the room where the correspondence books of the British Commander-in-Chief were held, and that he did not know what he meant by having papers already presumed to be secured in a small room collected. 'Am I to understand that this procedure meets with your disapproval? May I point out in no spirit of umbrage that specific and detailed instructions as to the operation of this Bureau are in fact...a reflection on my capacity as Officer-in-Charge.'[12] This incident is representative of what was evidently a general attitude of apathy and neglect towards the Military Archives from the greater portion of officers at the time.

J.J. 'GINGER' O'CONNELL TAKES OVER AS DIRECTOR OF INTELLIGENCE

Colonel J.J. O'Connell, one-time IRA Director of Training and National Army Deputy Chief of Staff, took over as Director of a below strength Second Bureau on 1 April 1929 and immediately set about its reorganisation. In November of 1929 he reported to the Chief of Staff that:

> A commencement was made in the matter of Archives. The documents existing here are in the process of arrangement: at the moment this will be slow, as it is not possible to assign anyone to it whole-time.[13]

The following month O'Connell updated the Chief of Staff that:

> In the matter of Archives a considerable amount of work has been done in the matter of taking over files dealing with the Civil War period, sorting out our own files etc... Certain files of no value to us have been set aside for transfer to the Civic Guard. I intend to inform General O'Duffy at once of these.[14]

By April the following year O'Connell had made significant progress, informing the Chief of Staff that:

> The principal new departure since my former Report has been in the matter of Military Archives. A considerable amount of progress has been made with reference to these, and the material here has been re-arranged in a more easily accessible form. Indexing and synopsising have also made appreciable progress. Measures are in preparation with a view to assembling material for a properly authoritative Official History of the War of Independence.[15]

A major difficulty faced by O'Connell and his staff was the ongoing one in connection with requests received for access to records which

Colonel MJ Costello, the Director of Intelligence responsible for the establishment of the Military Archives as a sub-section within Army Intelligence in 1924. *Credit: Major General MJ Costello Collection, The Military Archives.*

Left: Colonel JJ 'Ginger' O'Connell. The first formally appointed 'Officer-in-Charge' of the Military Archives, giving an on-site lecture on the history of the Battle of the Boyne. *Credit: Redston Collection, The Military Archives.*

Below: Notifications of a book overdue from the RDS Library. During his tenure Colonel JJ O'Connell personally incurred library fines for sourcing book for the use of the Military Archives. *Credit: The Military Archives.*

Royal Dublin Society.

TELEPHONE:
BALLSBRIDGE
61545.

LIBRARY.

Street : Ireland in 1921

is
~~are~~ now overdue, kindly return without delay.

J. F. GRAY,

Ball's Bridge, Dublin.   *Librarian.*

Right: Captain Alphonsus Blake, the Intelligence Staff Officer with responsibility for the Military Archives until 1926. *Credit: Image provided by John O'Byrne.*

Below: Lieutenant Colonel Niall Charles Harrington, Staff Officer at the Second Bureau and later the Military Archives. *Credit: The Military Archives.*

M I L I T A R Y   A R C H I V E S.

DRAFT OF PROPOSED
ESTABLISHMENT.

SUBMITTED HEREWITH to D.I.
in compliance with direc-
tion received verbally
11. 2. 25.

G.H.Q. PARKGATE, 19.2.25.

(Signed) Tomas O Gealbhain.

Above and opposite: Thomas Galvin's February 1925 Draft of Proposed Establishment of the Military Archives, a very significant foundational document. *Credit: The Military Archives.*

I.   O B J E C T I V E S.

a.   The custody of Military State Papers.

b.   Filing, Indexing and Cataloguing.

c.   Preserving the Records of the Service.

d.   Military Research.

e.   Relieving Departments of surplus files

f.   Reception of Papers contributed from private sources.

g.   Precis work.

"C" SECTION,

OUR REF. _____   INTELLIGENCE STAFF,

G. H. Q.

18th November, 1924.

TO/

The Director of Intelligence.

SUBJECT:- STATE DOCUMENTS
AND FORMATION OF
MILITARY ARCHIVES.

Sir,

As you are already aware this Section of the
Intelligence Staff have, amongst its other duties, been
labouring upon the collection of material for War Diaries,
Historical Calendars, and cognate matters. The materials
from which such works are being built up are largely
drawn from newspaper cuttings, Command Reports, Records of
Military Reports and Statistics Department, and Intelligence
Reports and Surveys.

The material available is necessarily small, and a
good deal of what is popularly called "scrounging" has been
resorted to in order to get some of it together; and the
time which this Section can devote to the work is also necessarily limited. These drawbacks are due to various
causes which it is not necessary to go into here; but the
importance of the work would be obvious to any person of
education who would examine the work done to date.

As a result of my continual search for further
material I learned that Mr. Galvin had a collection of documents in a room in the main building which he brought from
the Castle. I went across to see him, but as he was out I
did nothing beyond look at the covers of the volumes. To
say I was amazed at the amount of works, and their importance,
which had been gathered by, I believe, accident, is to mildly
express my feelings.

I arranged with Lt. Hayes of this Section to bring
over Mr. Galvin to see me; which he did. I learned from Mr.
Galvin (1) that he is only temporarily attached to Operations;
(2) that there is much more of the same documents in the
Castle under the temporary care of a man named Markam; (3)
that the "War Office" of the Castle is still intact, and was
not handed over to any Department definitely. I expressed my
astonishment at this, but was assured it was true.

Now the existence of these State Documents entirely
changes the complexion of the work this Section has been
doing in that direction. Their existence raises a very
important issue, and calls for a clear decision on the part of
superior authority. As the situation is at the moment the
entire collection might very easily be lost to the State.

(OVER)

Above and opposite: Commandant Brennan-Whitmore's November 1924 letter to the Director of Intelligence on State Documents and the Formation of Military Archives. *Credit: The Military Archives.*

Civilization has cursed the Vandals and the Goths for the
destruction of the early records and monuments of civilization;
and we as a Nation have cursed the Danes and the Norsemen for
the destruction of the early traces of Celtic civilization and
learning. But what will future generations of our race say of
us if, through our negligence, we allow invaluable State documents to be lost? That, in my personal opinion, is the exact
situation.

I put forward the opinion, with great respect, that all
State Documents, whether of the old regime or the new, which
have reached the historical stage - that is to say, are no
longer current - and relate to matters of Military interest,
should be in the care, and under the control of the Intelligence
Branch; that the Intelligence Branch should be charged with
setting up an Historical, or Military Archives, Section, and the
head of the Intelligence Branch charged with the care, preservation, and historical utility of every page.

I do not propose to go very deeply into the question
just now; but, if necessary, I am prepared to work out a scheme,
and to submit it. My duty at the moment is merely to seek to
raise the importance of the subject, and to seek a decision.

I asked Mr. Galvin to give me a List of Books and
Documents in his possession. I attach his memo., and whilst I
do not agree in toto with his arrangement of objects, I would
invite your attention to his "Sectional Index." It will at
once give you a clear idea of not only the historical, but the
military interest and importance of the collection. If, in
addition to this collection, there is really a "War Office"
store of books and documents still intact in the Castle, all I
can say is that their value is incalculable in terms of £.s.d.!

I am, Sir,

Your obedient servant,

W.J. Brennan-Whitmore Commandant.

OFFICER i/c. PRESS & SURVEY SECTION.

Encls.

*Note para 3. It is not true that Mr Galvin
brought the documents from the Castle.
They were "found" thrown into a
cellar in the main building.*

WJBW/KMcE.

OFFICE OF DIRECTOR OF INTELLIGENCE,

General Headquarters,

PARKGATE,

DUBLIN.   2nd December, 1924.

To/
  CHIEF OF STAFF.

Sir,
      Re: Historical documents and the formation of
                    military archives.

              I have the honour to bring to your notice
that the Press Survey Section of this Department has
for some time been devoting a certain amount of
attention to the collection of material for the compilation of War Diaries, Historical Calendars, etc.,
and in the course of their searches for such material
have recently discovered a quantity of very valuable
documents, most of which have reached the historical
stage, at present filed in an office under the charge
of Mr. Galvin and attached to Operations Department.
              We are also informed that the British "War Office"
in the Castle is still practically intact and contains
a quantity of similar documents of much value.
Apparently the War Office was never definitely handed
over to any Department and is at present under the
temporary care of a Mr. Markham.

              It is respectfully suggested that a proper
Military Historical Section should be set up into
which would be gathered all material of historical
value, including those papers at present in the custody
of Mr. Galvin, the "War Office" at the Castle, and
various material relating to the Republican Army, its
organisation and activities since 1916, which material
is at present in the hands of various officers and
civilians throughout the country.

              Such a Historical Section would be of very
great value and would provide a happy hunting ground
for editors of our Military Journals and for those of
our officers with a leaning for research work.

              As to what Department should be entrusted
with the collection and care of this Historical Section
is a matter for later consideration and decision, but
it would seem urgent that the material or "War Office"
at present in the Castle should be immediately taken
over by the Military Authorities.

                            I have the honour Sir, to be,
                            Your obedient servant,

                                              COLONEL.
                    DIRECTOR OF INTELLIGENCE.

  TK/JP:

Letter from Colonel MJ Costello to the Chief of Staff, December 1924, on Historical Documents and the Formation of Military Archives. *Credit: The Military
Archives.*

could assist the verification process required to progress Military Service Pension applications. On 1 July 1930, O'Connell wrote to the Chief Staff Officer, confirming that his staff were not in a position to verify pre-Truce service for the purpose of progressing such claims, stating that 'we have no records of the pre-Truce period and cannot verify the service of any man who claims to have served in the I.R.A. – a regrettable admission but unfortunately true.'[16] O'Connell also informed him that his department was not permitted to extend their research outside official circles and had not received 'official sanction or encouragement'[17] to actively acquire material connected to the pre-Truce period.

O'Connell assigned one of his Staff Officers, Captain Niall Charles Harrington, to the task of arranging archives and 'key records' held by the Bureau. The 'key records' identified by O'Connell were Civil War operation reports[18], intelligence records[19] and old British records[20] which constituted the bulk of the material held by the Military Archives at that time. In October 1930, O'Connell reported to the Chief of Staff that:

> Captain Harrington has made very important progress in this matter. In addition to old British Records the very voluminous operation records of the Civil War period have been gone into on a large scale. This work is being continued as speedily and fully as is possible in present conditions as Captain Harrington is only able to devote a portion of his time to it.[21]

O'Connell's progress with the Archives was interrupted when he proceeded on the Staff Officers Course at the Military College on 23 February 1931, and was temporarily replaced by Commandant Dan Bryan as Acting Director of the Bureau. Upon his return in late 1931 he found a Second Bureau that laboured under considerable difficulties in his absence. Bryan had had to devote a considerable amount of his time to interdepartmental committees with which he was associated, and during July and August was engaged full time on the preparation of returns for the World Disarmament Conference. The work of the Archives specifically was further frustrated and slowed up during this year by the absence of Captain Niall Harrington on a course at the Military College.[22] O'Connell was replaced as Director of the Second Bureau by Colonel Liam Archer, upon taking up his new appointment as the Officer-in-Charge of the Army Equitation School, on 9 March 1932.

LIAM ARCHER AND THE 1932 'BURN ORDER'

One of the first tasks overseen by Archer marks a dark period in the history of Irish archives, this being in response to the Destruction Order authorised by Desmond Fitzgerald, the Cumann na nGaedheal Minister for Defence, on 7 March 1932.[23] This Order directed the destruction by fire of all of the following classes of documents:

a. Intelligence Reports – including Reports and particulars supplied by Agents and other persons.
b. Secret Service Vouchers, etc.
c. Proceedings of Military Courts, including Committee of Officers. Reports on and details of Executions 1922–1923 period.

The reason given for the Destruction Order was that such documents contained information which could lead to loss of life if disclosed to unauthorised persons, and was given in the wake of the imminent hand-over of power to their previous Civil War opponents in Fianna Fáil, established by Eamon de Valera in 1926 following a split in Sinn Féin. While Fitzgerald's Order said that, prior to destroying these records, they were to extract such particulars that they considered might be required afterwards in the conduct of business of the Department of Defence, Archer noted that as a consequence of destruction, surviving files and documents required a 'complete overhaul.' It is unknown how much material was lost in the execution of the Destruction Order. Archer's staff did not succeed in completing an inventory as they had admirably endeavoured to do before the Order came into effect.

The Military Archives had been born, at least indirectly, out the flames of the Public Records Office at the outbreak of the Civil War. Through a combination of organisational necessity and personal interests it developed as part of, and parallel to, the Defence Forces during its first decade of existence, despite sometimes not fitting comfortably within the Second Bureau. Almost ten years later, in the destruction of these Civil War records, Ireland suffered another loss of records that could have provided invaluable insights into the difficult origins of the State.

Chapter 3

1933–1935: COLONEL E.V. O'CARROLL AND THE ANGLO-IRISH CONFLICT PROJECT

The Archives sub-section became known as the Historical Section during the tenure of Colonel Eamonn Vincent O'Carroll. This title reflected the orientation of the section towards actively compiling a history of the revolutionary period from those identified as reliable sources, namely, commissioned officers of the Army who had had pre-Truce experience. While this project never achieved the success that its instigators had envisioned, the associated documentary records now contained within the Military Archives' *Historical Section Collection* are a valuable resource in understanding the history and development of the Military Archives as an institution during this period.

O'Carroll was the Acting Director of the Second Bureau between 1933 and 1935. While he spent a relatively brief duration with the Second Bureau, O'Carroll's vision and enthusiasm for the work of the Historical Section paved the way for the formation of the Military Archives as it would be formally established in 1935.

COLONEL E.V. O'CARROLL

O'Carroll was born on 17 October 1893 at Meenahinish, Killygordon, County Donegal. A National Teacher by profession, he completed two years of university education before joining the Army. O'Carroll joined the Monaghan Brigade of the IRA in 1918 and, taking the pro-Treaty side during the Civil War, his service ran into the foundation of the National Army. He entered the National Army in February 1922 at Clones and was first appointed as Divisional Adjutant, and from September of that year as Officer Commanding, of the 5th Northern Division. He was officially commissioned into the National Army on 28 February 1923 and appointed Office Commanding Dundalk District, Dublin Command.

O'Carroll was first appointed as Director of the Second Bureau on 1 January 1926, and although he only held this position for a short period due to health issues, he earned a reputation as a pragmatic officer of very high standards.[1] Less than eight months into his first tenure as Director, in August 1926, the Director of Medical Services granted O'Carroll two months sick leave. O'Carroll was suffering from symptoms that included loss of appetite, depression, and lethargy. The Officer Commanding St Bricin's Military Hospital noted that O'Carroll appeared 'to be overworking at his office....'[2]

On 1 August 1927, on the direction of the Adjutant General, O'Carroll was posted as the Officer-in-Charge of Inspection Staff, while Colonel Frederick Henry succeeded him as Director of the Second Bureau. This episode did not prove to be a black mark on O'Carroll's career progression. Increasing evidence and appreciation of the psychological toll of the revolutionary years has come to light recently, not least via the records of the *Military Service (1916–1923) Pensions Collection*. In O'Carroll's case, both his personal testimony and that of his references in his pension application, record that he had been heavily involved at the coalface of active service during the War of Independence.[3] In his Annual Report for 1928 the Chief of Staff described O'Carroll in glowing terms:

Colonel Eamonn V O'Carroll is a very capable, hard-working, officer. He is exceptionally conscientious and has an unusually high sense of duty. He is quite capable of filling a higher appointment, and will be a success in any such appointment, as his extreme thoroughness, combined with his ability, enables him to get a complete grip of his work in a short time. His ambition is to make the Army an efficient fighting machine, and all his energies are concentrated on that end.[4]

O'Carroll proceeded to hold the noteworthy appointments of Adjutant General (from 4 June 1929) and then Acting Assistant Chief of Staff (from 4 June 1932). On 1 July 1932 he was appointed Director of the First Bureau (personnel) and on 9 September 1933 he was appointed Acting Director of the Second Bureau (intelligence) in the absence of the actual Director, Colonel Liam Archer, who had been temporarily posted to the Curragh to undertake a Command and Staff Course.

A PRECURSOR TO THE BUREAU OF MILITARY HISTORY

The *Anglo-Irish Conflict (1913–1921) Project* came about during a time when there was a growing awareness within political circles (particularly amongst Fianna Fáil, who had taken power in 1932) of the need to document the events of the Irish revolutionary period. It was, in many ways a precursor to the *Bureau of Military History (1913-1921)* in the 1940s and 50s, the origins of which date back to this same year of 1933. Minister for Education, Thomas Derrig, suggested to the Department of Defence initiating a project to collect and preserve the records of the War of Independence. These, he proposed, would take the form of witness statements which would be compiled and deposited at the National Library of Ireland. Derrig's proposals did not make any substantial headway until 1942 when Robert Dudley Edwards approached the Taoiseach, Éamon de Valera, about such a project and authored a memorandum on the subject on behalf of the Irish Committee on Historical Sciences.[5]

It was within this milieu of a growing awareness of the significance of the history of the revolutionary period, and capturing it before the memories of the participants faded, that the *Anglo Irish Conflict (1913–1921) Project* was conceived. Since its foundation the Army had used its official publication, *An tÓglách,* as a vehicle to document the events of the Rising and the War of Independence, but it 'fell foul of the Government…due to the forthrightness of its political and analytical contents'[6] and the last issue was published in 1933. The Army continued to attempt to collect such historical material through the Historical Section.

In a contextualising essay written specifically for the public release of the Bureau of Military History, Dr Eve Morrison noted that in the '1930s the Departments of Education and Defence both initiated schemes to collect personal testimonies through the medium of the Irish army' – which included the *Anglo-Irish Conflict Project* – as the Army 'was considered a natural choice to collect material and administer such a project,' though these attempts were rather unsystematic. Neither were they particularly inclusive, concentrating their efforts mainly on commissioned officers with pre-Truce service. Morrison also points out that 'the various configurations of the army schemes reflected changes in the political atmosphere and ethos of the times, as independent Ireland moved gradually away from the political hostility of the 1920s and 1930s spawned by the civil war.'[7] This point should be of particular interest to archivists, as the politicisation of archives is always cause for concern. While the modern archivist understands that the archive is an agent of accountability of the state, and advocacy for the people of that state, through the provision of access to the documentary evidence of the state's decision-making processes, these events took place well before the National Archives Act or the current extent of archival professionalisation. Archiving is 'an inherently political craft'[8] that is humanised by acknowledging our subjectivity. Nonetheless, it is interesting to observe the effects of political influence and societal context on the development of the Military Archives, and Irish archives in general, at that time.

INITIATING THE PROJECT

It was during O'Carroll's tenure that the Historical Section initiated the *Anglo-Irish Conflict Project* to collect historical written testimony connected to the 1913–1921 period. On 31 October 1933, O'Carroll wrote to the Chief of Staff, Major General Michael Brennan, to formally propose the project. In this letter, O'Carroll demonstrated a distinctly archival tendency in his solid comprehension of the value of preserving the testimony of the period beyond its immediate historiographical utility:

Sir, I have been considering the advisability of doing something in the collection of information from officers in the army regarding the work of the Volunteers from 1913–1921. My reason is not to collect data for the compilation of a history of the movement but rather to collect information before the sources are dead and gone and before the memories of officers become dim so that this information tabulated, say by counties or units, will be available for future historians in our military archives.

Col [Colonel] O'Connell QMG [Quartermaster General] made an attempt to do something on this line some years ago when he was in the 2nd Bureau, but Maj Gen [Major General Joseph] Sweeney, then C.S. [Chief of Staff], objected, and the thing came to naught. Personally, I am of the opinion that the project should have gone ahead as it would look bad on our part in the eyes of future historians if we allowed such sources of information to remain untapped.

I do not anticipate that we will do much of an ambitious nature, but even a modest start in the collection or mere cataloguing could be a good start and lay the foundations for our Historical Section which incidentally has never functioned as yet.

> Prior to raising the matter at a Staff meeting I would favour your views as there may be some reason for the original objection. If the matter does not meet with your approval then that will be an end to it.[9]

O'Carroll was pushing an open door. The Chief of Staff was very interested. As already mentioned, the history of the independence movement was topical within higher circles; there already existed support at Government level, and it seems that his letter was simply the formal initiation of the project. Brennan immediately replied to O'Carroll, telling him that:

> I think this is a very fine idea and you should go ahead with it at once. The President [of Dáil Éireann, Éamon de Valera] mentioned it to the Ministers and myself about a month ago and emphasised the opinion that we should get after it. There is no need to raise it as a Staff meeting.[10]

On 8 November 1933, O'Carroll wrote to the Officer-in-Charge of Personnel, based at the Department of Defence, Parkgate, requesting a list of serving regular officers with pre-Truce service in order to 'proceed with the procuring of information from serving officers as to the activities of the pre-Truce Volunteers in the areas in which they served.' O'Carroll's concluding remark in this letter that 'I am sorry to give you such a heavy job and if forwarding it piecemeal according as your Staff finds leisure to do it, will help you, I am quite agreeable'[11] does not suggest that this project was considered as a top priority for the wider Army, despite having both de Valera's and Brennan's blessings. It is certainly indicative of a section that worked, as Commandant Peter Young observed many decades later, 'in fits and starts'[12] and where the 'officers appointed were normally seconded to other duties considered more pressing at the time.'[13]

By the middle of January 1934, O'Carroll was ready to begin, and circulated several hundred copies of his request for accounts. In his letter he informed the officers of the Army that:

It has been decided that the Historical Section of the Second Bureau will proceed with the collection of data for an official History of the period 1913–1921, i.e., from the formation of the Volunteers until the signing of the Truce in 1921.

It is not intended that the Second Bureau will write this History, but merely that the information collected will be catalogued for the use of future historians…Incidents, no matter how seemingly unimportant, should be included. In addition to such information you may be in possession of documents, old newspapers, etc., or have knowledge of some less known persons with valuable information. All of these will be of assistance and will be very welcome.

It is not suggested or intended that documents, which must naturally have great sentimental value for the possessor, should be handed over to the Second Bureau. It will suffice if a catalogue is made of these documents and the nature of the information they can furnish indicated…[14]

LIEUTENANT COLONEL NIALL CHARLES HARRINGTON

Correspondence in relation to this project was primarily dealt with by Niall Charles Harrington, who at the time held the rank of Captain, on behalf of O'Carroll, as one of his Staff Officers at the Second Bureau. Along with Colonels M.J. Costello, E.V. O'Carroll and J.J. O'Connell, he was one of the four leading officers responsible for the development of the Military Archives between the 1920s and 1940s.

Harrington was born in Dublin on 23 January 1901. His father was the well-known Timothy Harrington, Member of Parliament, Barrister, first President of the Keating Branch of the Gaelic League and, at that time, the Irish-speaking Lord Mayor of Dublin. Harrington, like Costello, O'Connell and O'Carroll, had pre-Truce service with the Irish Volunteers. A chemist by civilian profession, Harrington joined the Volunteers in 1919 and held the rank of Lieutenant in 'A' Company of the 1st (Boyle) Battalion, of the North

Roscommon Brigade. A year later he also joined the Irish Republican Brotherhood (IRB).

On 8 March 1922, soon after the signing of the Anglo-Irish Treaty, he was attested into the newly established National Army at Beggars Bush Barracks as a Private in the Medical Corps. By April he attained the rank of Corporal and by June the rank of Sergeant. During the Civil War he served in his capacity as a medical NCO at the siege of the Four Courts and the following month was posted to Kilorglin, County Kerry, as part of a National Army endeavour to rout heavily entrenched anti-Treaty forces in the area, transferring to the Dublin Guards during this time. He was promoted to the rank of Second Lieutenant in August 1922 for gallantry at the Droum Ambush. Harrington also gave testimony to the Court of Inquiry into the Ballyseedy massacre, during which Free State troops, under General Paddy O'Daly, used landmines to kill IRA prisoners.

Harrington first entered the story of the Military Archives in 1926, when he was posted as a Staff Officer to the Second Bureau, by this time holding the rank of Captain. Harrington had worked previously under O'Carroll during his initial posting as Director of the Second Bureau from 1926–1927.

THE ANGLO-IRISH CONFLICT PROJECT

On 18 January 1934, Lieutenant Fred Slater, based at the Artillery Barracks in Kildare, replied to O'Carroll's circular to apologise that 'the only incident worthy of recounting that I could give anything like a detailed account of would be of the capture and burning of Belleek RIC Barracks which took place on the 5 September 1920.' In his reply Harrington demonstrated that, like O'Carroll, he understood the purpose of the project beyond mere hagiography. Writing to Slater the following day he reassured him that 'we are anxious to obtain all the information possible concerning Volunteer activities during the period, and information furnished from several sources regarding a particular incident will help to ensure historical accuracy.'[15]

This was a healthy approach. Even in the 1930s, competing narratives about events during the revolutionary periods were in circulation, with certain antagonists even taking their quarrels to the press. This is illustrated, for example, in Captain S. Hayes letter to Harrington dated 18 January 1934, when he wrote to express his inability to provide an accurate historical account as requested by O'Carroll, but informing him that:

> A history (to which reference was made some time ago in the 'Irish Press') was compiled by Mr T. O'Duffy of Navan and I will endeavour to secure for you a copy of this. I understand that Mr P. Giles of Trim is also about to complete some similar history as he has intimated that in a letter published recently in the 'Drogheda Independent' that the record compiled by Mr O' Duffy is distorted.'[16]

The initial responses were far from numerous but seemed promising. Typical replies, such as that from Captain Andrew Lohan, also of the Second Bureau, told Harrington that 'I intend shortly to commence the work of compiling information concerning the escapades and incidents which occurred in the area of my activities.'[17] When exactly he could expect to receive the accounts of such 'escapades' was another matter. Similarly, Lieutenant Thomas Giblin's reply that he would 'proceed with the compilation of my account on the subject as soon as possible'[18] was typical of the vagueness of the majority of the responses that did arrive on Harrington's desk.

Others were simply too busy, including Colonel Liam Archer, the Director of the Second Bureau in whose place O'Carroll was then acting. He replied from the Military College that 'as far as I can see I can not undertake this task until the termination of this course.'[19] A minority made no pretence at all. Captain M.F. Dodd of the Army Medical Service sent a straightforward reply to O'Carroll that he was simply 'not in a position to give first-hand information on the events of that period'[20] despite having been identified as an officer with pre-Truce experience. Similarly, Lieutenant Seán Moroney, of 4th Infantry Battalion, Collins Barracks, Cork, replied that 'I regret having to inform you that I have very little information of any note at present.'[21] At least they took the time to reply.

The correspondence from early 1934 also shows that the reliability of memory was already starting to become an issue, a significant point considering that this project preceded the *Bureau of Military History* by over a decade. Major General Joseph Sweeney, General Officer Commanding the Curragh District, agreed to 'put on paper a record of as many incidents as I can remember having occurred in the area of the 1st Northern Division' with the caveat that 'naturally, after so many years one forgets much of what happened and I have no records left as they were all captured shortly before the Truce.'[22] Similarly Captain P.J. O'Rourke, Admin Officer, 7th Infantry Reserve Battalion, replied expressing his concern that 'it is difficult to remember dates back 18 or 20 years but every possible effort will be made by me to ascertain the correct dates of the various engagements and incidents that took place in my Battalion Area.'[23]

Some of the early responses were fruitful, even if falling short of providing the actual accounts requested. For example, O'Carroll's circular turned up a map in the possession of a Corporal Seán Ó'Muireasáin, of 1st Infantry Battalion, Galway, which had been captured by a Cork Flying Column from British Forces and showed IRA areas as visualised by the British authorities from captured documents and secret service reports.

The letters of acknowledgement from Commandant John B. McDonald, Military College, Pearse Barracks, Lieutenant Patrick J. Kelly, 2nd Infantry Battalion, Portobello Barracks, and Captain M.J. O'Brien of the Air Corps, show that O'Carroll's was not the only contemporary project of its kind either. All three referred to a project being undertaken by former members of 'E' Company, 2nd Battalion, Dublin Brigade IRA, being spearheaded by Liam Daly. In his letter, McDonald informed O'Carroll that:

Ex-Commandant William Byrne, ex-Commandant Jim O'Neill, and ex-Captain Liam Daly, old officers of E Coy, 2nd Battalion, Dublin Brigade have been considering for years the advisability of gathering together members of the company for the purpose of collecting data for a history of the Company during the period 1913–1921.

I was speaking to Liam Daly (who was Company Adjutant for a number of years) yesterday and he informed me that he had already begun the work and had some documents. He suggested that if members were brought together that a more accurate account of the company's activities could be given and I understood from him that the work of bringing the members together had begun.[24]

Captain M.J. O'Brien subsequently informed O'Carroll that Commandant McDonald 'gave me to understand that as soon as this work is completed it will be forwarded to your Department.'[25] However, whether such a history was ever completed, or if it exists in an identifiable, discrete form is uncertain. It certainly does not exist within the material of the Historical Section at the Military Archives. Perhaps an indication lies within Daly's statement to the Bureau of Military History sixteen years later, in which he recounted that:

My next and last contact with Seán [Russell] was in 1933, when I wrote him asking his co-operation in compiling a history of 'E' Company, 2nd Battalion. The letter I got in reply further emphasised my realisation of sixteen years earlier. In it he says, 'I am sorry I cannot co-operate in your scheme, as the work for which 'E' Company was formed has not yet been accomplished. Therefore, no history of this Company can be complete until its aims are attained.'[26]

In the end, the initial positivity was deceptive. O'Carroll and Harrington did not receive the responses that they had hoped for or that the project required. On 9 February 1934, Harrington cast his net further, writing again to the Officer-in-Charge of Personnel on behalf of O'Carroll, now requesting a list of reserve officers' names with pre-Truce service. He received a list of thirty-seven officers of the Reserve of Officers with 1916 Service, the majority of whom had taken part in Easter Week, and invited them to make submissions to the project. On 5 April 1934, O'Carroll circulated a reminder letter informing recipients that 'the personal reminiscences of officers who participated in the 1916 Rising is particularly desired at present in order to assist the work of compiling an official history of the Rising by the Department of Education.'[27] This parallel collaborative project was being undertaken at the time and sixteen of these accounts are currently held at the National Library of Ireland.[28]

On 17 April 1934, O'Carroll wrote to the Chief of Staff to inform him that, despite the circular letter to both Regular and Reserve Officers, and the large number of replies stating that they would furnish him with the information as soon as possible, at the time of his writing only two detailed accounts had been received.[29] The Chief of Staff was not impressed. He immediately circulated a letter for the attention of the Assistant Chief of Staff, Adjutant General, Quartermaster General, all Bureau and Corps Directors, and the Provost Marshal, expressing his disappointment at the lack of participation by the men under their command.

> I wish to refer to the efforts being made by the Historical Section of the Second Bureau to obtain the personal reminiscences of officers who participated in the Anglo-Irish Conflict, and to express my regret at the poor response to this effort. In January last all officers of the Regular and Reserve forces who had pre-Truce service were circularised and asked to prepare an account of the history and activities of the Volunteer Units in which they served. The purpose of this request was fully explained in this circular letter to which I refer and it is a matter of concern that the appeal did not receive the support it merited. A very large number of officers did not even acknowledge receipt of the circular and altogether only seven actually sent in written narratives.
>
> There would seem to be some unaccountable reason for this lack of enthusiasm and hesitancy about furnishing the information asked for.

Will you please take steps to impress upon the officers under your command the national importance of this work and the absolute necessity of compiling these personal reminiscences before the passage of time removes valuable source of information.

The object of the undertaking is the collection of information regarding the Volunteer Movement before sources become extinct. The information collected will be tabulated and stored in the Military Archives for the use of future historians. The accounts when received will be housed in the Military Archives for the use of reputable historians and will not, at any time, be available for idle perusal by the merely curious.[30]

This unambiguous encouragement from the Chief of Staff had some effect, ostensibly at least. The Reserve of Officers proved a particularly fruitful avenue, with a few members replying in the affirmative and expressing their eagerness to help. In relation to privately held documents, one reserve officer contacted Harrington offering items of interest including: an original coded telegram in relation to a warning of a break in the Truce and the date and time of its termination; a British order detailing action to be taken on termination of the Truce; a British intelligence map showing IRA Brigade and division boundaries; and British defence orders for the Royal Hospital Kilmainham, 1921.

O'CARROLL DEPARTS, ARCHER RETURNS

On 19 July 1934, O'Carroll was transferred from the appointment of Acting Director of the Second Bureau and attached to the Army's General Staff, where his tasks involved presiding over several boards, including Procurement of Armoured Vehicles and Interviews for Commissions in the Volunteer Reserve. It is here that his role in the story of the Military Archives ends, going on to higher offices and by 1940 holding the rank of Major General.

On 22 November 1934, Colonel Liam Archer, now back as the Director of the Second Bureau, wrote to his Staff Officers informing them that:

I desire to draw your attention to the attached letter from the Chief of Staff. It should not be necessary to point out to officers of this bureau how desirable it is to place on record their experiences during a period of such great historical importance. Your daily work shows you that reference to such records of personal experience is the only satisfactory method of compiling information of any real value. I expect therefore that all officers will comply with the request of the C.S. [Chief of Staff][31]

With Archer's support, the project carried on into 1935, with Harrington providing both the ability and the continuity needed. While he had an unambiguous understanding of the importance of collecting as broad an array of accounts as possible, his personal experience and understanding of the 1913–1921 period meant that he was not beyond subjectively identifying and pursuing accounts of incidents deemed of particular significance. One notable and interesting example is Harrington's letter of 13 September 1935, to Lieutenant Denis Begley (Reserve of Officers at that time), who had been involved in the shooting of British agent Lieutenant Henry James Angliss on Bloody Sunday 1920, in which he is unmistakably eager to secure Begley's account:

Dear Denis,

No doubt you are aware that a Military Archives has been set up and from that you may deduce that the 'old hands' will soon be pursued for their histories. I don't seem to recall that you replied to our earlier circular sent out some time ago? But you should try sometime to jot down any information you can think of or whatever recurs to your mind from time to time. At the moment I am deadly anxious to obtain the story of Frank Teeling's rescue from Kilmainham Gaol in 1921. You know the whole story! – the secret plans and how they were successfully carried out. Will you let me have it? I am engaged in the compilation of Regimental Histories – a more or less brief outline of Irish Military History from the Danish invasion to our own day. At the moment I am dealing with the Dublin Regiment (Volunteers) and have reached the period of the 3rd Volunteer Convention in 1917. I can only mention most incidents in brief outline; some not at all, but others I wish to give prominence to and of course acknowledge the source of the information in the bibliography of the hand-book. Will you help me out in the matter of Frank Teeling's rescue Denis? I will facilitate you in any way you wish – by arranging to meet you here in my office or elsewhere and take notes myself in long hand; or by providing a short-hand note-taker who will take down the story as you tell it and so save you the trouble of writing it. On the other hand if you prefer to write it yourself I will wait your convenience. The important thing is that I want to get the story and will look forward to hearing from you or seeing you.[32]

Two things may strike readers as peculiar about this letter. The first is Harrington's tone – one of enthusiasm bordering almost on desperation. It must have been becoming clear at this stage that despite the encouragement of the Chief of Staff the *Anglo Irish Conflict Project* was not going to achieve the success that O'Carroll and Harrington envisioned. There are a very small number of written testimonies amongst the material in the Military Archives' *Historical Section Collection* but nothing close to constituting the resource initially envisioned for the project.

The second thing that may strike readers as peculiar is Harrington's statement to Begley that 'a Military Archives has been set up.' What he is referring to is the first establishment of the Military Archives as part of the official strength and organisation of the Army, as a discrete entity within the Intelligence branch, as opposed to a fluctuating sub-section, a 'historical section' or, in a more general sense, as simply a physical repository of military records.

This was not the only important change to occur in 1935. The official establishment of the Military Archives required the appointment of an Officer-in-Charge, and this appointment was given to Colonel J.J. 'Ginger' O'Connell.

Chapter 4

1935–1978: RISE AND FALL – THE COLONEL J.J. 'GINGER' O'CONNELL YEARS AND AFTER

olonel J.J. O'Connell returned to the Second Bureau in 1935, having held the appointment of Quartermaster General (a Colonel's appointment in those days) since June 1932, and was appointed as the Officer-in-Charge of the Military Archives. Despite the existence of the Military Archives in forms discussed previously he was the first officer to officially hold that title as a formally established one. During his tenure, from 1935 until his sudden death in 1944, he would become the single greatest influence on the development of the Military Archives prior to its disestablishment in 1959 and laid the foundations for the work of Commandant Peter Young following its resurrection in the 1980s. O'Connell's journey from Volunteer leader to Deputy Chief of Staff of the National Army, to the first Officer-in-Charge of the Military Archives is worthy of a broad biographical description as it is one of both serendipity and misfortune, and one which most significantly defined the development of the Military Archives.

J.J. 'GINGER' O'CONNELL

In the introduction to his transcription of *Colonel J.J. O'Connell's Memoir of the Irish Volunteers, 1913–1917*, Dr Daithí Ó Corráin noted that 'no one had a longer high-ranking association with the Irish Volunteers and successor Irish armed forces than Jeremiah Joseph O'Connell'[1] but surprisingly little has been comprehensively written about his life and times. It seems that Ó Corráin's article, along with Dr Marie Coleman's account in the *Dictionary of Irish Biography*, as well as his mention in various third-party historical accounts and Bureau of Military History Witness Statements are the sum total of his biography. Colonel Tom Hodson (retired) recently attempted writing a biography of O'Connell but finding sources sufficient for an entire book proved too difficult. At the time of writing, the project has been scaled back to an extended essay.

Jeremiah Joseph 'Ginger' O'Connell was born 21 December 1887 at Ballina, County Mayo. His pre-National Army service is a matter of well-known historical record but is relevant to the story of the Military Archives in order to appreciate both the wealth of experience and ability he brought to the institution, as well as helping to understand something of the man himself and his frustration at being demoted from General to Colonel after the Civil War, a rank beyond which he was never to be promoted again.

Having earned a first-class Master of Arts degree from University College Dublin he served in the United States Army's 69th (New York Irish) Regiment between 1912 and 1914. While this is a period about which very little is known, it is reasonably suspected that O'Connell deserted. In her witness statement to the Bureau of Military History, Cumann na mBan member Josephine MacNeill claimed that 'on the outbreak of war he had deserted from the American Army as he felt that the time was opportune to return and help organise resistance against the British in his own land.'[2]

O'Connell joined the Irish Volunteers in 1914. During 1915-1916, he was the Volunteers' Chief of Inspection, holding the rank of Commandant. This role involved organising Volunteer units and giving lectures on military tactics. The job also included regularly contributing to the *Irish Volunteer*, the organisation's official publication. This newspaper was used to communicate orders and directions to the Volunteers, as a training and educational tool that disseminated instruction and articles on drill and operational matters, as well as reporting on the activities of the other Irish nationalist organisations, Cumann na mBan and Fianna Éireann.

It was O'Connell, along with Bulmer Hobson, who accompanied Eoin MacNeill when he confronted Patrick Pearse on Holy Thursday 1916, upon discovering that the mobilisation orders for Easter Sunday was actually a cover for an IRB-instigated rebellion, and he was subsequently tasked with circulating MacNeill's countermanding order. Following the Easter Rising, in which he was not directly involved in the combat, O'Connell was imprisoned from April to December 1916 at Wandsworth, Frongoch and Reading. While at Frongoch he played a key leadership and training role amongst the Volunteers, ensuring military ethos and discipline was instilled and morale was maintained.

Following his release, he took up an appointment as an instructor with the Sligo Brigade IRA and was imprisoned again in 1918, this time in Gloucester jail. He was released in 1919 and by 1920 he was appointed at the IRA's Director of Training, following the death of Dick McKee in custody that November. O'Connell appears in Leo Whelan's well-known painting *IRA GHQ Staff, 1921,* as Assistant Chief of Staff, Whelan having seized the opportunity to paint it when the Truce provided a window during which the members of GHQ could finally appear in public. In 1921 he took part in the Anglo-Irish Treaty negotiations in London as part of the committee dealing with defence.

Over the course of the Treaty negotiations, de Valera had complained to Collins and Griffith that O'Connell had been appointed to the delegation without having referred first to the Minister for Defence, Cathal Brugha. According to Tim Pat Coogan, this complaint was, in fact, part of the wider machinations of de Valera, along with Brugha, to use O'Connell in a plan to create a New Army, which would involve the officers and men being discharged and re-commissioned / re-enlisted with a new oath of allegiance to Dáil Éireann. Richard Mulcahy was instructed by Collins to call a meeting with GHQ to discuss the matter, and as a result the entire GHQ objected to de Valera's plans and so they did not come to pass. This caused de Valera to lose his temper at having been out-manoeuvred. O'Connell was, of course, numbered amongst those objecting members of GHQ, describing them as a 'band of brothers' that needed no such reorganisation.[3]

By February 1922, O'Connell held the rank of Lieutenant General and the appointment of Deputy Chief of Staff, responsible for training and organisation, in the new National Army. At this time the fault lines were appearing between the pro-Treaty Army and the anti-Treaty IRA, foreshadowing the Civil War that was to come. On 18 January 1922, the Minister for Defence, General Richard Mulcahy, called a meeting of GHQ and senior commanders, and scheduled an Army Convention for March in order to try to reconcile the pro- and anti-Treaty sides. While Mulcahy and Collins, recently appointed Chairman of the Provisional Government, were supporters of the Treaty, they took a reconciliatory approach towards their erstwhile comrades on the anti-Treaty side. Throughout this period, for example, Collins was still working behind the scenes with the anti-Treaty IRA to continue the war in Northern Ireland and protect Catholics against Protestant pogroms. There were instances of the National Army arming the anti-Treaty IRA with Lee Enfield rifles, with the National Army having been supplied them in turn by the British.[4]

During 1922, O'Connell's attitude to the anti-Treaty IRA was uncompromising and hard-line, in contrast to Collins' more conciliatory approach, and significant given the previously mentioned use by Collins of the anti-Treaty IRA to keep the fight going in the North. In

Tim Pat Coogan's biography of Michael Collins he observed that the popular O'Connell was deliberately identified to be kidnapped on the orders of Rory O'Conner in retaliation for the arrest of Leo Henderson, a prominent anti-Treaty IRA man garrisoned at the Four Courts during its occupation, by the Provisional Government.[5] According to John Dorney, 'the timing of the Henderson arrest was probably deliberate provocation.'[6] Depending on your perspective the kidnapping of O'Connell on 26 June 1922 either forced the hand of the Provisional Government or provided a *casus belli,* and in the early hours of 28 June the National Army began shelling the Four Courts and the Civil War had begun.

In the period after his release from the Four Courts, O'Connell was given the new appointment of Director of Inspections and later General Officer Commanding the Curragh Camp. During the 1923 army reorganisation, in which O'Connell was reduced in rank to Major General, Mulcahy loyalists were given key appointments. O'Connell was certainly not as close with Mulcahy as he had been to Collins. Some of these men were well known to Mulcahy as fellow members of the newly revived Irish Republican Brotherhood's (IRB) Supreme Council, and in his subsequent testimony to the Army Enquiry Committee in 1924 O'Connell commented on how the majority of such positions were deliberately filled by Mulcahy from the ranks of the IRB,[7] while conversely many who had been loyal to Collins were put out to pasture. This was not necessarily a bad thing; one of Mulcahy's greatest concerns was with Army Intelligence which was comprised of many former Squad men who had become a law unto themselves, with their ill-discipline going as far as conducting summary executions.[8] While he was a Collins loyalist, O'Connell was consummately professional and believed that there could be no place for secret societies within the Army.[9]

Mulcahy was not the only prominent person about whom O'Connell had been critical. David McCullagh has noted that, as Director of Inspections in 1916, immediately prior to the Easter Rising, O'Connell had described the 3rd Battalion of the Dublin Brigade, commanded by Éamon De Valera, as 'much the weakest in the matter of command'[10] in comparison to the other three battalions. While he was careful in this report not to put the blame on any one individual but rather on circumstances, all military commanders are aware that they bear full responsibility for everything those under their command do and fail to do. His connection to the Rising was a key aspect of de Valera's political and personal identity so it is a reasonable hypothesis that this was not something a man of his particular character would quickly forget.

FALLEN OUT OF FAVOUR?

Both Mulcahy and de Valera remained highly influential men who had long careers in Irish public life after the Civil War, and Mulcahy at least would have had many supporters within the officer ranks of the Army. Very often, the long-term consequences of chosen courses of action do not become evident until seen as part of the totality of a lifetime, just as the individual threads of a tapestry seen from behind appear to begin and end arbitrarily until viewed in its entirety from the front. While this is speculative, evidence would suggest that somewhere along the line – be it in his criticism of de Valera's military prowess in 1916, his role and affiliation during the Treaty negotiations, his loyalty to GHQ over de Valera's and Brugha's designs on it, or his uncompromising attitude towards the anti-Treaty IRA during 1922 and the run up to the Civil War – O'Connell fell out of favour with some powerful people. It may be conjectured that this ultimately contributed to his demotion to Major General during the Army reorganisation in 1923 and then to Colonel in 1924, but the fact remains that, despite his protestations and representations, it was a rank above which he would never be promoted again for the duration of his military career.

Or perhaps it was something more mundane? O'Connell never held a command appointment in either the Volunteers of the National Army until he was appointed General Officer Commanding the Curragh

Camp, and he was quickly relieved of this command. In O'Connell's 1935 annual performance appraisal the Chief of Staff, Major General Michael Brennan, described him as 'an officer of great ability but rather more academic than executive or administrative.'[11] Perhaps, and again this is somewhat hypothetical, while he was clearly a man of incredible ability with so much to offer the Volunteer movement, the rigid structures of a National Army or the rigours of the life of a soldier, may not have been the ideal environment for his particular abilities to express their full potential at the highest level.

O'Connell's losses in terms of career advancement and appointment to the General Staff meant that his proven skills and energy would contribute most significantly to the establishment of the Military Archives in its formative years, initially during his posting as Director of the Second Bureau between April 1929 and March 1932 and more significantly as the first officer to hold the formally established appointment of Officer-in-Charge in 1935.

While he fulfilled this role with the enthusiasm and zeal one would expect from someone with his experience and ability, he was not without ambition for promotion to higher rank. His disappointment at his position is evident in a letter he wrote in 1927 to the Chief of Staff, Lieutenant General Peadar MacMahon, while O'Connell was Chief Lecturer at the Army School of Instruction in the Curragh. There is a tone of insistence in this letter, something plaintiff even, that suggests O'Connell indeed felt that he had fallen out of favour but was unaware exactly why or how:

In the event of the promotion of any Colonels to the rank of Major-General I respectfully claim that my name should appear first on any such list of promoted Colonels. This would be the simple, automatic result of applying the principle of Seniority. Seniority is the accepted way of promotion for an Army Officer except in the event of his displaying gross incompetence or neglect of duty. If there is any suggestion that I have been guilty of either I respectfully ask that a Court of Inquiry be convened with a view to establishing the same. My seniority rights are based on the following:

    (a) Having formerly held the rank of a general Officer.

    (b) Having been a member of the Volunteer Executive in 1915.

    (c) Having been a member of the Pro-Truce GHQ Staff.

In the event of written proof being required to establish any of these I am in a position to furnish such proof.

As regards my reduction three years ago to the rank of Colonel I acquiesced at that time in a definitely accomplished fact. I never intended that such acquiescence should be regarded as renouncing all rights to being again promoted when any new promotions were being made under normal circumstances like the present.

Since being reduced I have done my best to perform all military work assigned to me in the rank of Colonel: I am not conscious of having seriously failed in my duties at this rank. I, therefore, submit that since I was reduced to the rank of Colonel I have not been guilty of any military fault of a nature to prejudice my promotion.

I respectfully ask that this matter should receive full consideration now, in order to prevent any misunderstanding, the whole question having been recently raised by certain statements in the public press.[12]

Any direct official objection or obstruction to O'Connell's promotion is difficult to identify. Major General Joseph Sweeney, in O'Connell's *Annual Confidential Report 1927–1928,* described his skills as the Chief Instructor at the Army School of Instruction in glowing terms: 'most painstaking when on practical demonstration' and 'after hours always ready to give any help required.' Regarding O'Connell's intellectual and academic prowess, Sweeney noted that because of his 'good written and spoken knowledge of French [he] is able to profit from ideas in French Military Journals and Manuals and articles of his bearing on Military matters have appeared in some of the important French periodicals.' He closed his report with the opinion that he had 'no objection to his promotion in the normal course.'[13] Whatever 'the normal course' was for a man of O'Connell's experience is somewhat ambiguous and something upon which Sweeney did not elucidate.

O'CONNELL'S FIRST BRUSH WITH THE ARCHIVES

On 1 April 1929, O'Connell was appointed as the Director of the Second Bureau, later and more widely known as 'G2'. In the following year's annual confidential report Sweeney commented that 'during the year Colonel O'Connell has shown himself to be conscientious and capable, and has been engaged in laying the foundations of military archives.'[14] This is the first reference on file to O'Connell's role with the archives, but he was not alone. He had with him for help a Staff Officer who would also play an important part in the development of the Military Archives and whom O'Connell described in his first annual report as his Commanding Officer as 'able, conscientious and hard-working.' In this assessment he recorded that this officer had 'recently completely rearranged the very numerous files of the Second Bureau and thereby greatly facilitated matters of reference' and noted that he was 'at present engaged in arranging the Archives and has made considerable progress in this,' remarking that in both of these tasks he had 'displayed considerable initiative.'[15] O'Connell's able assistant was the previously mentioned Captain Niall Charles Harrington, who was transferred from his appointment as *Staff Officer, Second Bureau* to *Staff Officer, Military Archives* in 1935.

ESTABLISHING THE MILITARY ARCHIVES

O'Connell was appointed as the first Officer-in-Charge of the Military Archives on 4 June 1935 and immediately set about establishing precisely what duties this new position entailed, and equally important, where exactly those duties were to be performed. On Saturday 8 June, O'Connell inspected the office accommodation at the Red House – the

Second Bureau headquarters at Infirmary Road, Dublin – as a potential location. He noted that the top floor was occupied entirely by the Second Bureau and that there was no room whatsoever available there. On the middle floor, the Second Bureau occupied a small office; the rest of the floor was occupied by the typing office and the rest of the rooms by the Director of Engineers and his staff, which O'Connell described as already cramped. The ground floor, O'Connell noted, was inhabited by Engineers and Artillery in similarly cramped office space. At that time, all of the archive papers were contained in one storeroom, which O'Connell described as adequate for the moment but overall, he considered the Red House to be entirely unsatisfactory. On 11 June 1935, O'Connell wrote to the Chief of Staff with a better proposition:

> In all circumstances I am satisfied that the best solution at the moment is to open new offices in Griffith Barracks. Two could be opened at once and others added – say one for each period – as necessity arose. Later on, when the additions to Parkgate [Army Headquarters] are finished, more space will be vacant in the Red House and the entire service can be concentrated there. It would, in my opinion, be a serious handicap to an entirely new Service to require it to function from the start in too crowded surroundings.[16]

Griffith Barracks, on Dublin's South Circular Road, was the best option as far as location was concerned. Following on from his letter of the 11 June pointing out the practically insurmountable difficulties in the way of securing suitable office accommodation at Parkgate, O'Connell inspected Griffith Barracks and reported positively to the Chief of Staff that suitable accommodation existed there.

> This exists at the present time – without disturbing any office now occupied – in the shape of a set of four rooms close together. Two of these are spacious, well-lighted rooms suitable for offices and connected by a floor between them. The other two rooms are suitable for filing-rooms, and either of them is as large as the store now taken up by the archives behind

the Red House. A very minor adjustment of existing offices would set free another excellent room if such were required. Altogether the accommodation is far superior to anything I suspected to exist in Griffith Barracks.[17]

O'Connell left the Chief of Staff in no doubt that he was anxious to start work no later than the following week, requesting his permission to formally occupy the offices at once. Permission was forthcoming, but as well as the new location, O'Connell's appointment was a brand new one to the Army establishment and he had no formal instructions regarding his duties and responsibilities. He wrote to the Chief of Staff asking for 'a more precise indication of the duties of my new appointment... At the moment there is nothing in existing Regulations or Instructions to serve as a guide.'[18] The Chief of Staff's reply was vague:

As your appointment is an entirely new one is it not possible at this stage to indicate precisely what your new duties will be. The main object is, as you are aware, to collect Irish military historical material particularly for the period 1913–1921. As you have considerable experience of historical research you will be able to suggest the best lines on which your office should be developed. I propose making Captain Niall C Harrington available for your staff (in addition to Capt Murphy) and handing over to you all our available historical documents including, of course, the Kilmainham Papers[19]

LIMITED RESOURCES

The Military Archives was now formally established and operational. O'Connell took up the position with the intention of applying the same initiative and zeal that had characterised him as a leading figure during the revolutionary period to this new appointment and intended to excel. By the time the Military Archives had occupied its new real estate in Griffith Barracks, O'Connell had already prepared an outline scheme of how the Archives would collect material from the 1913–1921 period for the information of the Chief of Staff, covering the main headings of *Easter Week, reorganisation of the Volunteers after 1916*, and *operations from 1920–1921*. He also took the opportunity to request additional staff, in the person of Sergeant Doyle, who had been engaged on the work of the archives for a long time previously.[20]

Despite the establishment of a brand-new Colonel's appointment of Officer-in-Charge for the Military Archives, resources remained a difficulty. On 25 November 1935, O'Connell wrote to the Chief of Staff explaining that since the establishment of the Military Archives a few months previously, a considerable volume of typing had accumulated and that he was badly in need of a typist. While there was, at that time, a typist employed in Griffith Barracks who would do some work in their spare time for the Military Archives, it was insufficient for the Archives' requirements. O'Connell categorically informed the Chief of Staff that the Archives had far too much work on its own and that to regard it as of secondary importance to the work of another branch was out of the question:

> We have, as you will understand, many interviews with people who were predominant in the struggle for independence. That is an important part of our work, and the information so gained has to be typed, submitted for approval to the person concerned, and then retyped. All this takes time, but it is essential to ensure historical accuracy.[21]

The Military Archives required a significant amount of associated correspondence and administrative work, further compounded by the fact that Harrington had just authored his *Volunteer Handbook of the Dublin Regiment,* which also had to be typed and submitted.

On this issue, O'Connell had limited success. The Military Archives was given the use of a typist but only between 2 p.m. and 5 p.m. daily, on the authority of W.P. Blunden of the Army Finance Office, an experienced civil servant who had been in the Department since 1924, working under the previously mentioned C.B. O'Connor. In his note to O'Connell on 18 November 1935, Blunden informed him that all of this work was to take place in room F2 as it was 'most undesirable that a type-writing machine be constantly shifted about.'[22] While it may seem laughable in the modern era, it gives some indication of the relative inconvenience of the typewriter as an instrument at the time.

In what was arguably a case of the Department of Defence not seeing the wood for the trees, the typewriter issue dragged on into 1936, with O'Connell arguing the case for a typist and typewriter throughout the early part of that year. Petitioning the Adjutant General, applications were opened for a typist clerk position at the Military Archives and seven were subsequently received. In April 1936, O'Connell received an addition to his staff in the person of Private Joseph Deignan, originally from Forkill, County Armagh, who he had deemed as the most suitable applicant and who was transferred from the 2nd Battalion, Regiment of Rifles, based at Portobello Barracks.[23] It was a minor victory and in October that year, trying to build on his small but hard-won success, O'Connell wrote again to the Establishment officer, Mr Taylor, seeking a second typewriter.

While the difficulties placed in the way of O'Connell in procuring resources as essential to the work of the Military Archives as typewriters and typists may seem short-sighted or petty, it was not historically uncharacteristic of the Department of Defence in its relationship with the Defence Forces. This is what Professor Eunan O'Halpin described as a 'control by starvation philosophy.'[24] This tight control over even meagre sums is also illustrated in the difficulties of O'Connell in procuring things as straightforward as books for the new Military Archives.

During 1936, the Military Archives produced reference bibliographies of publications pertinent to 1916 and to the 1912–1921 period, as well as identifying books for purchase. The Archives had become, in many ways, a historical research endeavour, so one would assume books would have been an essential requirement. Currently, however, O'Connell was incurring fines from the library of the Royal Dublin Society (RDS) for overdue books, as he was borrowing titles on his personal membership for the purpose of the work of the Military Archives. One letter from O'Connell to the Chief of Staff, dated 21 October 1936, reminded him of the matter of a request for £5 for the purchase of books. He pointed out that until then he had been using his RDS membership to borrow books for the Archive's purposes, something that he rightly described as wholly unsatisfactory. It is a sad indictment of the half-hearted support of the Department of Defence to the work of the Military Archives at that time that O'Connell felt the need to give assurance that he was 'prepared to give the fullest accounting satisfaction as far as concerns the portion of the £5 expended'[25] – less than €300 in today's money.

The Chief of Staff forwarded the request to the Secretary of the Department of Defence, C.B. O'Connor, who parsimoniously recommended that any books required by the Military Archives be purchased by Colonel Archer as the Director of the Second Bureau, deposited in the central library and borrowed by O'Connell. This was impractical, bearing in mind that the Second Bureau and the Military Archives were in different locations at that time. There is no mention of any additional funding being made available to the Second Bureau for the procurement of books required by the Military Archives, but documents record Harrington sourcing a selection of second-hand books from England in December of 1936. It seems that the intention of the Departmental Secretary was that the money would come from the Second Bureau's budget.

The matter still carried on into 1937. On 4 February, J.J. O'Connell wrote to Colonel Archer informing him that:

I have already discussed the matter with the Chief of Staff and explained that we are forced to beg and borrow books from private sources and public libraries in order to get material for our files and for the preparation of reports, memoranda etc. All this material should be available in our office because it is an essential part of our sources of reference and, as you will readily understand, having such sources on hand, we would be saved a considerable amount of time spent in the National Library and elsewhere.[26]

While this constant fight for resources demonstrates a lack of vision and ambition by the Department of Defence, O'Connell's relentless fight to make sure that the Military Archives excelled in its mission illustrates that he was undoubtedly a man with clear aspirations and dogged determination to ensure the success of the Military Archives. His was a vision that went far beyond typewriters and books.

O'CONNELL'S VISION FOR THE MILITARY ARCHIVES

On 24 August 1936, having just received his typist, O'Connell wrote again to the Chief of Staff, with a much more extensive set of recommendations and requests for the Military Archives. Owing to the gradual extension of the work of the Archives, O'Connell informed the Chief of Staff that he now found it necessary to ask for additional staff, and to seek a definite separate establishment for the Military Archives as a military section of the Department of Defence, distinct entirely from the Second Bureau. The following extract from this letter presents O'Connell's own words on the matter:

> As you are of course aware the Military Archives was formed in June 1935 with the express design of collecting and recording all the material possible connected with the War of Independence from 1913–1921. Shortly after its formation offices were established at Griffith Barracks and I moved in there with my staff which consisted of Captain Harrington and Sergeant Doyle both of whom belonged, and still belong, indeed, to G2 Intelligence Branch.
>
> At the outset we were burdened with a quite formidable array of files and documents which had to be removed from the Department of Defence to our new offices at Griffith Barracks. These documents are not

of a nature particularly related to our work since they consist for the most part of Army and Civil War records, but they are nevertheless documents which would eventually find their way to the Military Archives, and their removal and rearrangement in our stores is work which we might ordinarily expect. The work, however, is not by any means complete as there are still several thousands of documents of particular importance in the basement at the Department of Defence which have to be brought here and dealt with. The whole matter, both as regards the documents taken over and those awaiting transfer, requires a great deal more attention than can be given to it by the present limited staff. A further matter which involved a considerable amount of time and trouble was the transfer of the 'Kilmainham Papers' to the National Library. These papers had to be suitably arranged and checked before being handed over but the matter has since been finally disposed of.

Meanwhile, we were concerned with the primary function of the branch, – the collection of material connected with the War of Independence. In this we can claim to have made satisfactory progress: we have established a system of filing and card index record: we have carried out much research work in the National Library and elsewhere, and we have had many interviews with people and made contact with others whose help should prove valuable later on. Our work has now reached a stage when expansion becomes necessary and in order to cope with the work ahead we must be provided with adequate staff and a properly constituted unit or branch.

During recent weeks we received an addition to our staff in the person of a soldier Clerk-Typist, a Pte Deignan, transferred from the 2nd Battalion R.O.R [Regiment of Rifles]. Unfortunately Deignan has ceased to draw additional pay since his transfer owing to the fact that we have no separate establishment of our own. The position is unfair and unnecessary and, furthermore, the other members of my staff Captain Harrington and Sergeant Doyle are still borne on the strength of the G2 Intelligence Branch.

You will appreciate, therefore, I feel sure, the necessity for having the whole position adjusted by the establishment of the Military Archives on a properly constituted footing. I propose the following establishment for your consideration and approval:

1 Colonel: Director
1 Commandant
2 Captains
2 Sergeants
2 Corporals
1 Private

The sub-division of duties shall be as follows:-

(1)   The Commandant to function as Deputy to the Director and in this capacity to assist in the more important work of personal interviews, research work, editing of documents and authentication of information.

(2)   1 Captain for reading, research and classification of information, and for photographic work throughout

(3)   1 Captain for administrative duties in the Branch, office routine, correspondence, filing, cataloguing, indexing, and control of staff.

(4)   1 Sergeant (clerk) as assistant to No.2 in research and photographic work.

(5)   1 Sergeant (clerk) as assistant to No.3 and principally to take charge of stores and the care and preservation of documents.

(6)   2 Corporals (clerks) both of whom shall be typists.

(7)   1 Private (clerk) for general copying work and runner.

This would be an addition of 2 officers (captains), 1 sergeant, 1 corporal and 1 private to my present staff. I am desirous of having Captain Harrington permanently attached here to act as Commandant as he is in every way suitable for the rank and appointment and later I expect to be in a position to supply the names of other suitable personnel.

The foregoing establishment is essential for the proper functioning of the Military Archives. Our work is of a varied and even tedious nature and we must have sufficiency of staff in order to cover the ground necessary. Furthermore, we must have the backing and resources of a properly organised military branch of the Department of Defence and the only way to do this is to provide a separate establishment for the Military Archives.

I trust you will approve of this proposal and I ask particularly to have the matter dealt with at an early date.[27]

Unfortunately, but unsurprisingly, O'Connell's requests were not acceded to, but again, like Béaslaí before him, he understood the true value of the work and acted as its committed advocate. Like the challenges of post-Civil War demobilisation and reductions faced by Béaslaí, the Defence Forces was at that time at the tail end of a process of reducing the numbers of regular troops and increasing the numbers of reservists, which had been borne out of the 1926 Army Organisation Board report. The shortcomings of this policy would, of course, become vividly apparent with the outbreak of war in Europe in 1939. If the Archives were not to reach their full potential – from lack of funding, staffing, equipping or interest – it would not be for want of effort on the part of O'Connell. By formally submitting letters such at this, neither could those in authority claim ignorance as a defence or mitigation to their responsibility.

BUILDING THE MILITARY ARCHIVES' COLLECTIONS

While O'Connell spent a lot of time and energy during the first year engaged in internal wrangling to put the Military Archives in the best position possible to carry out its mission, he was also looking to build the Archives' collections from various sources both within and outside of the Army. By 1935, it was becoming clear to O'Connell that the *Anglo-Irish Conflict Project* was not going to be as successful as initially envisioned by E.V. O'Carroll. Despite the project falling flat, O'Connell still targeted those best placed to provide information, namely, those members of the Army with pre-1922 service. He did not only concentrate on the

Volunteers either. In January 1936 for example, O'Connell wrote to the Assistant Chief of Staff, Aodh MacNeill, requesting that he be put in touch with any accessible sources, oral or written, relating to Fianna Éireann and the early phases of cooperation between them and the Volunteers:

> Sir, as the Fianna was the first really military Institution in Ireland in recent times, I am very anxious to get as full and authentic information as possible about its institution and growth. By 'Military Institution' I mean a body undergoing military training and learning the use of arms – which, I think, the Fianna did as early as 1908 or 1909.[28]

The result was a comprehensive memo and summary of Fianna operations[29] compiled by MacNeill himself, quite possibly the first attempt to compile a history of that organisation. More significantly, this was an important recognition by the Army of the very important role played by Fianna Éireann in assisting the Volunteers after their formation, as well as their participation in the Easter Rising, with two of their number, Commandants Seán Heuston and Con Colbert, being executed by the British in the aftermath.

It was not only organisations with republican credentials that were of interest to the Military Archives either. Dossiers from that time also exist within the *Historical Section Collection* in relation to the British Army and the Ulster Volunteer Force,[30] the latter formed by northern unionists to oppose Home Rule by force of arms. These records appear to be typed transcriptions and as well as the subject of the UVF, they record the 'Manifesto from the Grand Lodge of Ireland' (Orange, not Masonic) and the strengths and locations of various UVF regiments and battalions.

While useful historical dossiers, these were still secondary sources. In June 1935, O'Connell wrote to the Chief of Staff and informed him that 'as a result of the recent consideration and assessment of sources for the History of 1913–1921 period, I have come to the conclusion that the most valuable existing source at the moment is constituted by the 1924

Pensions Files.'[31] O'Connell's keen appraisal of these records foreshadowed the *Military Service (1916–1923) Pensions Collection* by over seventy years, but perhaps even he could not have guessed that these files, as well as those for pensions awarded under subsequent acts, would become the single most important source of documentary evidence for the revolutionary period to the extent that they have. However, recognising that the pensions' files could not be used for this purpose for many years to come, he perused other avenues.

Later that year, O'Connell identified old 'Commander-in-Chief' files that were located in Army Headquarters as suitable material for the Military Archives and wrote to the Chief of Staff. Captain Sean O'Neill, the Personal Staff Officer to the Chief of Staff, replied that:

> The matter has been discussed with the secretary and there is no objection to the taking over. Files which are considered proper to G2 should be passed to that particular branch. Regarding the burning of worthless files, the Chief of Staff considers they should be left aside and their disposal afterwards considered.[32]

The attitude to the 'burning of worthless files' may seem offhand or even negligent, particularly to those familiar with the National Archives of Ireland Act 1986 and its provisions for the preservation of state records for public inspection. Such throwaway comments, however, provide an insight into how records at that time could potentially be arbitrarily disposed of with little oversight. We can never know the full extent of records from that period that did not survive and must remain mindful of the fact that no archival collection is really 'complete.'

1936 – LOOKING OUTWARD

O'Connell began 1936 by writing to Dr T.J. Kiernan, the newly-appointed Director of Radio Éireann, based at the General Post Office

(GPO) in Dublin. Informing him of how the Military Archives had been primarily established for the purpose of gathering as much information as possible about the period of the Anglo-Irish Conflict, O'Connell successfully requested from Kiernan a script of recently broadcast talks on the subject of prison escapes as a useful source of first-hand information. Kiernan put O'Connell in touch with the broadcaster Noel Harnett, who in turn asked O'Connell if he knew of any other successful escapes that had not been covered in a series he had been producing if he could let him know.[33]

O'Connell's letter of reply to Harnett on 13 January 1936 is interesting for two reasons. Firstly, it demonstrates the tentative beginnings of the Military Archives outreach activities; external public engagement remained a key tool of advocacy for the archives under Commandant Peter Young in the eighties and nineties, and it remains a core function of the institution today. Secondly, it demonstrates O'Connell's enthusiasm and distinctive suitability of character for the appointment of OIC Military Archives.

In his letter, O'Connell discussed in entertaining detail some of the various methods that IRA members had employed during the revolutionary years to furnish their escape from captivity. Such methods included: using passes obtained from sympathetic members of the Board of Works employed at the camp; escaping in swill carts and laundry carts; and hiding under a load of timber in the back of a truck. One particularly amusing anecdote concerned a man who managed to reach the road some distance from the prison camp and stow away in the back of a slow-moving delivery van. Soon afterwards, the van stopped and the driver opened the back doors to make a delivery. To the escapee's horror he found himself outside the Curragh Camp headquarters. Fortunately, the driver was sympathetic and provided the escapee with an overcoat, and the two delivered parcels together to the Officers' Mess![34] O'Connell's deep and genuine interest in his appointment shines through in this letter.

THE KILMAINHAM PAPERS

During May 1936, O'Connell was in correspondence with Sir Henry McAnally in relation to the latter's request to access *The Kilmainham Papers. The Kilmainham Papers*, discussed in an earlier chapter, originated from the administration and correspondence of the Commander of British Forces in Ireland, dating from 1780–1894. The papers were transferred to the Ministry of Defence upon the evacuation of British Forces in 1922 and were subsequently transferred to the National Library of Ireland by the Military Archives in 1936, in hindsight a tremendous loss to the Military Archives but understandable given the focus during that time on the 1913–1921 period.

McAnally's letter dated 4 May 1936 enquired whether the Papers would be located at Kilmainham or if they were to be prepared and moved to the National Library by the time of his visit to Dublin the following month. He signed off 'with many thanks for your very courteous staff,' a minor detail but illustrative of the positive public reception to the work of O'Connell and his small team.[35]

O'Connell's reply to McAnally is not on file but a fair approximation of its contents can be made from McAnally's subsequent reply four days later when he wrote, 'if I might have the pleasure of seeing you on June 2nd - that would be very agreeable to me.'[36] In McAnally's subsequent article on the subject of the Kilmainham Papers in the *Journal of the Society for Army Historical Research* he thanked O'Connell and Harrington for putting their knowledge of the collection at his disposal. It is very obvious that both O'Connell and Harrington were becoming acknowledged as serious players within the Irish archival landscape.

GINGER'S POPULARITY – THE HUMAN FACTOR

While 'Ginger' O'Connell's success was greatly due to his very significant organisational and intellectual aptitudes, his personality also contributed to both his individual success and to that of the Military Archives under his leadership. It is widely noted in various history books that O'Connell's popularity was partly the reason why he was kidnapped by the anti-Treaty Four Courts Garrison at the beginning of the Civil War. He never lost this popularity either. On 4 July 1939, he was invited to give a radio talk on George Washington during a special Independence Day broadcast, and on the twelfth, he gave one on the Battle of the Boyne. Archiving is a uniquely human practice, and the *human factor* is critical to the successful management of an archive. In modern professional archival practice, the self-conceptualisation of *the archival profession* is inextricably linked to the practicalities of archival management and the understanding that it is a profession characterised by several uniquely human and interdisciplinary facets. Decades before archival academics were publishing articles on this, O'Connell understood it intrinsically.

1939 – THE BEGINNING OF THE END

The year 1939 and the beginning of the Second World War – or 'the Emergency' as it was known in Ireland, a name derived from the Emergency Powers Act and the penultimate preparatory phase prior to invasion and the declaration of a full state of war – was the beginning of the end for the Military Archives. Niall Harrington, now a Commandant, was appointed as the Officer Commanding the Coast Watching Depot, an essential element of Ireland's rapidly introduced defence plans. In 1940, O'Connell was detailed by the Chief of Staff, Major General Dan McKenna, to carry out a study of general defence plans. This was an important responsibility in a world at war and one indicative of O'Connell's competency. It was, however, also a responsibility that only left him able to look after the Military Archives in a supervisory capacity.

This all took its toll on O'Connell, including on his health. By 1943, the Chief of Staff remarked that, while O'Connell remained deeply devoted to duty, tactful, loyal, diligent and faithful, his appearance and military bearing had become 'slovenly', and he was appraised as being 'not suitable' for an appointment in command of troops or for promotion to higher rank.[37] All of this was symptomatic of a man in decline. Tragically and prematurely, aged only 56, O'Connell died from a heart attack on 19 February 1944.

In 1946, the material held by the Military Archives at Griffith Barracks was transferred back to the custody of the Intelligence Branch.[38] While some archival work did take place during the latter part of the 1940s, including the cataloguing of the Collins Papers, much of the work of the Archives was, by this time, in support to the Bureau of Military History.

The Bureau was established on 1 January 1947 by the Minister for Defence, Oscar Traynor. Its stated objective was 'to assemble and co-ordinate material to form the basis for the compilation of the history of the movement for Independence from the formation of the Irish Volunteers on 25 November 1913 to the 11 July 1921.' Under Michael McDunphy as its Director, the Bureau was administered by the Defence Forces and staffed by a combination of military and civilian personnel including several leading historians. Between 1947–1957, the Bureau's team of investigating officers recorded 1,773 witness statements from people who had taken part in military activities during the 1913–1921 period.

Illustrative of the Military Archives supporting role, the papers of George Walsh for example, who had been a member of the Ancient Order of Hibernians and one of eighteen members who, in 1914, voted to co-opt John Redmond's nominees on the Irish Volunteer Executive, were catalogued and transferred to the Bureau of Military History. It is recorded that 'some papers regarded as being of outstanding historical interest, are retained as museum specimens for the Archives Section.'[39] This consideration of papers as 'museum specimens' is certainly suggestive of a loss of the understanding of the Archives holdings as dynamic items of documentary evidence.

It seems, however, that in general the Defence Forces care of historical documents was becoming very poor. In 1948, the Director of

Intelligence, Colonel Dan Bryan, issued a circular letter expressing his concern that:

> It has come to notice that in some instances historical documents not in current use or not likely to be required administratively are being carelessly disposed of. Indeed, some have been destroyed outright without due regard to their possible value at a later date, and recently certain records required by a corps for historical purposes were found to have been destroyed.
>
> When it is desired to dispose of official documents, destruction should only be resorted to where the papers concerned are of a purely routine nature and where, besides being of a routine character, they can be classed as valueless for record of historical purposes at any future date.[40]

In this letter, Bryan went on to explain that, where doubt arises as to the historical interest of any papers or other documents, reference should be made to the Officer-in-Charge of the Military Archives, 'who will afford all possible guidance and, where necessary, inspect the documents' and that any 'existing "dumps" of documents should also be reported to Officer-in-Charge Archives with as full particulars as possible.' Bryan himself was proactive in the identification and preservation of valuable records. One of the richest and most insightful collections of Emergency period records held at the Military Archives, the Army Intelligence *G2* and *G2X* series of files survived because of his foresight and direct intervention.

While Bryan's letter directed people to the Officer-in-Charge of Military Archives, the problem was, of course, that the appointment was very much defunct by that stage for any practical purposes. From 1946 to 1953, while Harrington officially filled the appointment of Staff Officer in the Archives Sub-Section (and therefore de facto Officer-in-Charge), he was never actually employed in this role. In reality, he performed the duties of Officer-in-Charge of the Security Sub-Section. Captain Gerard Shane Cox was appointed as Staff Officer, Archives Sub-Section, in November 1947, where he remained until 1954 and his promotion to Commandant. Due to a medical condition, he was medically graded as only suited for administrative appointments (a decision to which he objected and appealed), so his posting to the Archives was not primarily inspired by the same historical zeal as O'Connell or Harrington. Nonetheless, he was regarded as keen, intelligent, well-read, and well-informed by his Commanding Officer, Colonel Dan Bryan. Again, during his tenure, short staffing and other commitments deemed more pressing meant that he, like Harrington, was not engaged on the work of the archives full-time.

In 1953, Harrington was promoted to Lieutenant Colonel, but by this stage the Military Archives had become dormant. By 1959, the year of Harrington's retirement, the Military Archives was removed from the official establishment of the Defence Forces in the reorganisation of that year.

1959 – THE END OF THE BEGINNING

The reorganisation of the Defence Forces, which was implemented on 1 October 1959, saw the disestablishment of the Archives sub-section as the organisation was steered in a different direction with new priorities. This reorganisation reflected the exigencies of the Cold War and was premised around developing what was termed a Mobilisation Establishment, consisting of a Field Force of six Brigades with a Second Line Reserve of local troops giving a total of fifteen Battalions.

The 1958 *Memorandum to the Government on the Reorganisation of the Defence Forces* came on the back of several previous, and generally limp, attempts to make the force fit-for-purpose since the end of the Emergency. At this stage the geopolitical landscape had changed; it was the Cold War and the 1944 Scheme was no longer appropriate, never mind being unimplementable. Ireland had been something of a pariah as a result of its policy of neutrality during the War. In 1946 the League of Nations had been disbanded and Russia had vetoed Ireland's membership of the UN, established the previous year, until 1955. Ireland left the Commonwealth in 1949 (becoming a republic) and would not join NATO at least in part as it would be a tacit acceptance of British forces in Northern Ireland and partition. This 1959 Reorganisation was based around the most likely threat to Ireland's neutrality coming very soon after the beginning of hostilities between NATO and the Soviet Union, with Ireland regarded as being of potential strategic value to either side.[41] With this new focus for the Defence Forces, the Military Archives came to be considered surplus to requirement and was removed from the official establishment.

Over a decade later, Colonel Dan Bryan's 1948 letter remained the only definite instruction relating to the care of historical documents in force in the Defence Forces. Lieutenant Colonel P.P. Ó Neill, a successor of Bryan as the Director of Intelligence, noted in a 1971 letter to the Chief of Staff that:

> In 1967, a survey of the contents of the Military Archives revealed that a considerable amount of Emergency and Post Emergency material was stored there and that the latest addition was historical material re: the Defence Forces in the Congo and Cyprus. This would seem to indicate that the terms of the attached instruction [Bryan's 1948 circular] are still being adhered to.
>
> It might be noted that in line with Government Directive to an tAire Cosanta [Minister for Defence] dated 26 Meitheamh [June] 1946, there was provision for a military staff for duty in Archives up to 1959. But provision of this military staff was not included in the 1959 Peace Establishment. Since then some work has been done in classifying, registering and indexing some of the material in Archives by Mr [Patrick] Brennan [secretary] of an Buró Staire Mileata [Bureau of Military History] in 1962 and by Mr Bolger of an Roinn Cosanta [Department of Defence] in 1967. Since 1967 however, there has been no appointment of any indi-

vidual of staff, military or civilian, with the specific duty of attending the Military Archives. There is now NO military establishment for this purpose. S.Fais [Director of Intelligence] only retains the custody of these documents but has no staff available for the cataloguing etc. which is apparently necessary or suitably trained to determine whether documents are of historical importance or not.

An element of urgency arises if the 50 year ban normally imposed on the publication on release of official documents will cease to operate in 1972 for papers for the 1922 period. Apparently, much work remains to be done in cataloguing these papers if the custodians are to avoid criticism when such release takes place.[42]

With concerns evident in this letter about the impending potential release of records from the Civil War period and the *ad hoc* nature of the Defence Forces record-keeping and archiving practices, the need for a professional, functional archives service was clear. However, that apparatus – itself never *fully* realised – had been dismantled through years of neglect. This was the condition of the Military Archives when, in 1976, a new officer came along and took upon himself the arduous task of its reconstruction.

Chapter 5

1982–1990: THE COMMANDANT PETER YOUNG YEARS (PART 1)

On Friday 16 December 2016, the Reading Room of the new Military Archives building in Cathal Brugha Barracks was bustling. The annual Christmas coffee morning (more accurately, *Irish* coffee morning) had attracted its usual eclectic mix – friends and family, serving and retired soldiers, civil and public servants, academics, journalists, historians, archivists, a few descendants of famous revolutionary names and even the odd retired politician. The coffee morning is a special occasion; a chance for those who have been involved with the Military Archives throughout the year, or over the years, to get together with the Officer-in-Charge and the Archives' team, catch up and mark the beginning of the Christmas festivities. This year's coffee morning, the first in the Military Archives' new purpose-built facility, which had been officially opened only the previous April, was extra special. Among the attendees on this auspicious morning were many members of the 43rd Cadet Class. Alongside members of his family, they were there to mark the official dedication of the Reading Room in honour of one of their classmates – the man granted the epithet of 'the Father of the Military Archives.' That man was Commandant Peter Young.

1950–1975: EARLY LIFE AND CAREER

Peter Young was born on 15 June 1950 and lived at 29 Screen Road in Cabra, Dublin. He attended secondary school at Rockwell College, a prestigious boarding school in Cashel, County Tipperary, where he earned a reputation as a keen rugby player. Young graduated from Rockwell in 1967 and was accepted into the 43rd Cadet Class, which began training in the Military College, Curragh Camp, on 15 October 1968. In an assessment of Young by the headmaster of Rockwell College, required by the Cadet School at that time, his loyalty and self-confidence were rated very favourably. Upon being offered a place in the Cadet School Peter replied that 'I accept it readily, but humbly, with the hope that I will justify your faith and trust in me.' This faith and trust he undoubtably justified, featuring ten years later and holding the army rank of captain, among its notable alumni in the 1977 Rockwell College Annual.

In his chosen profession, Young followed in the proud military tradition of his father, Commandant Peter J. Young, who died in 1953 while Peter was a small child. Peter Young senior was born in Cork in 1904 and served with the 1st Cork Brigade IRA from 1918 to 1922. During the Emergency-period he was the Transport Officer of the Army's 2nd Division and in 1942 he had the substantial responsibility of mobilising all the Division's transport for the move south as part of the Blackwater Manoeuvres, which remain to this day the largest military mobilisation ever conducted by the Irish state.

Young was commissioned as a second-lieutenant and gazetted as Assistant Adjutant, 12th Infantry Battalion, Clonmel, on 28 September 1970. Very soon after he was posted to 1st Infantry Battalion in Renmore, Galway. It was here, at St Patrick's garrison church, located just outside the barracks gates, that he married Annette Dunne on 25 March 1972.

Young's first few years of military life were not unusual for a young army officer, but they were certainly eventful. He was involved with training various recruit platoons between 1972 and 1976 as well as undertaking three-month postings to the Northern Ireland border in 1972 and 1974. This was, of course, during the three-decade period of ethno-nationalist conflict known as the Troubles. Throughout these postings Young was in command of a platoon (approximately thirty soldiers), responsible for conducting duties in aid to the Garda Síochána - patrols, check points, searches – and the administration of military posts.

In October 1973, now holding the rank of full lieutenant, Young departed on his first overseas mission. This was as a platoon commander in the Sinai Desert, as part of the United Nations Emergency Force (UNEF) mission. Here, aged only 23, he was involved not only with the supervision of a platoon of thirty-five men but also in dealing with other United Nations contingents and negotiating at local level with Israeli forces to arrange ceasefires and safe passage of friendly forces, and the reporting of military incidents back to UN Headquarters.

Young returned to Ireland the following May and on 31 July 1974 he found himself, once again, undertaking a three-month posting to the Northern Irish border. It was here that he first met a journalist with whom he would become good friends, and with whom his path would later cross as both Assistant Defence Forces Press Officer and as the Officer-in-Charge of the Military Archives. That journalist was Robert Fisk.

In an interview for this book Fisk described how, during the 1970s, not a lot of British reporters spoke to Irish military sources.[1] Fisk recalled that he had 'thought there was an interesting story on the southern side of the border' and his first time on the southern side of the border with the Irish Army was in the company of Commandant Vincent Savino. Savino had been the Officer-in-Charge of the Defence Forces' Press and Publicity Sub-Section, part of the Intelligence Branch, from November 1972 until March 1978. Fisk first reported on Northern Ireland during the Loyalist Workers Strike, which took place in May 1974. It was soon afterward that Fisk first met Young, who had been appointed to accompany him around the areas of Coleman's Island and Clones in the border county of Monaghan. While during 1974 Young was still officially posted in the appointment of platoon commander, Fisk recalls that Savino had taken an interest in Young and groomed him for the Assistant Press Officer role, which he would officially assume in 1976.

From their initial meeting, Young and Fisk remained in contact. An incident which occurred the following year illustrates Young's competence and discretion as an army officer, and the trust a journalist of the calibre of Fisk placed in him gives an external perspective on the character of the man who would soon afterwards become the driving force behind the revival of the Military Archives.

Fisk recounted an incident in February 1975, when an official document was posted to his home by a Lisburn-based British Army intelligence officer from the 39th Infantry Brigade by the name of Captain Colin Wallace. Wallace would later be framed for manslaughter, believed to be for his refusal to participate in sordid smear campaigns against British politicians, and for attempting to draw public attention to the Kincora Boys Home sexual abuse scandal. The document he sent to Fisk revealed how the British Government had been planning to entrap and blackmail Democratic Unionist Party (DUP) members in sex scandals and, as it transpired later, this was in fact in connection with the events at the MI5 infiltrated Kincora Boys Home.

Fisk had initially met Wallace in a bar, where Wallace had told him the story of the intended entrapment. Fisk, of course, informed Wallace that he needed evidence to substantiate this claim before he could go to print. This duly arrived shortly afterwards. Fortuitously, Fisk had travelled briefly to London to meet with his chief sub-editor at the *Times* and, while he was away, Wallace posted a document containing the evidence through the letter box of Fisk's home on Harrys Road, Hillsborough, in county Antrim. The house, however, was being covertly watched by the security forces, who had been using Wallace in this instance in an attempted set-up and had assumed that they could orchestrate finding the document in Fisk's possession. Fisk was, of course, *persona non grata* with the British security forces at that time due to his refusal to kowtow to the establishment and his scrupulous reporting of their ignominious conduct. They were unaware, however, that he happened to be in London at that time.

Fisk's house-cleaner, whether by coincidence or design, happened to be the wife of a member of the Royal Ulster Constabulary (RUC). Fisk recalled that, when it transpired he was not at home, the cleaner was asked by the security forces to pick up the document and pass it on to her husband. The following day, 6 February 1975, the RUC and British Army arrived at the door of the recently returned Fisk's home. One of the RUC men approached Fisk with the document in an envelope and asked him if he had seen it before. Fisk pithily informed him 'of course not, it's in an envelope.' At that point the policeman revealed just the top of the document, exposing that the paper was headed 'SPO'. This was the abbreviation of Senior Press Officer, the appointment held by Captain Colin Wallace.

Fisk was asked to attend Belfast's notorious Castlereagh Holding Centre – the subject of many cases of police brutality – for question-ing. Fisk, naturally, smelled a rat and got himself immediately south of the border and into the Republic. He stopped at a public phone-box in Balbriggan while en route to Dublin in order to make a call to Charles Douglas-Home, who was Home Editor of *The Times* at that time. Home's response to Fisk upon hearing about his situation was 'thank God you've gotten out and you're safe in the South'. Douglas-Home then instructed Fisk to just cover the Republic from then on. Upon arriving in Dublin, he checked into Jury's hotel in Ballsbridge and telephoned two people. The first was Jonathan Swift in the Department of Foreign Affairs. The second was Captain Peter Young.

Shortly after arriving at the hotel, Fisk recalled being visited by Michael Daly from the British Embassy in Dublin. Daly wanted to speak to Fisk and suggested that they do so in his room. Rightly cautious, Fisk refused, insisting that they could speak in the lobby. Here, Daly accused him of 'having property belonging to her Britannic Majesty's Government.' Fisk refused to be intimidated, and immediately went to the Horseshoe Bar at the Shelbourne Hotel, for his arranged rendezvous with Peter Young, where he explained his situation. Upon mentioning his meeting with Daly, Fisk recalled Young informing him that he was, in fact, a senior British intelligence officer based at the embassy – a matter that was subsequently raised in the Westminster parliament[2] as well as in Tim Pat-Coogan's book *The Troubles*. Young reassured Fisk that he would be safe, telling him to 'deal first with the Department of Foreign Affairs, and then with me.' He told Fisk that he could call him at any time, at home or in the Red House, where the Irish Army's Intelligence Branch was based at that time, the Army Press Office falling within that branch. The Taoiseach, Garret Fitzgerald, subsequently intervened, and Fisk's subsequent career is, of course, a matter of public record.

This was not the last time Fisk and Young would cross paths, but these subsequent collaborations would be with Peter in his capacity as the Officer-in-Charge of the Military Archives. The incident related above, while being in one way tangential to the story of the Military Archives, was the one that cemented the relationship between Young and Fisk and is typically illustrative of the level of trust and professional competence associated with Young. As Fisk described it: 'We trusted each other about the North; I would tell him what I thought was going on, and Peter would do the same in return.'

1976–1982: ASSISTANT DEFENCE FORCES PRESS OFFICER

In 1976, Young was officially gazetted into the appointment of Assistant Defence Forces Press Officer. This he described as a most challenging appointment, which saw him dealing with the media on a daily basis. It also entailed close liaison with the Secretariat of the Department of Defence, the Government Information Services, and the Garda Press Office. There were two Press Officers at that time, and Young's particular day-to-day responsibilities were dynamic. He was responsible for the overall administration of the Press Office including preparing press releases, arranging press conferences, and briefing and escorting media representatives on visits to military installations.

Young's real passion during this time, however, was the Military Archives, and as soon as he had a foot in the door with the Press and Publicity Sub-Section, he began the campaign to have the Military Archives re-established. As Assistant Press Officer, one of his duties included dealing with historical queries. He soon discovered that military archives were at that stage basically non-existent. A 1977 article in *An Cosantóir* by Commandant P.D. O'Donnell, on *How to Research a Barrack History*, indicated the sparsity of the archives as a historical resource at that time. 'Army Archives' appeared without any further elaboration as a sub-heading within a short paragraph describing the resources available at Army Headquarters. Meanwhile the 'National Library,' the 'State Papers Office,' 'Old Books,' 'Living People' and even 'the United Kingdom' commanded greater column inches in his assessment.[3]

Young was proactive and, in response, enrolled in the diploma in Archival Studies in UCD between 1976-1977. The fees for this course were covered from the Defence budget, so at least Young was not alone in his appreciation of the importance of the preservation of Irish military documentary heritage. In 1977, he published an article in *An Cosantóir* entitled 'Military Archives in the Defence Forces'. In this, he tackled the absence of military records, inferred by O'Donnell's article in the same issue:

Any person who has had occasion to seek information on the Army or who has attempted to write a history of their unit will appreciate the difficulties in locating source material. The maintenance and preservation of military documents is one area that has largely been neglected over the years. An Archives Sub-Section did exist in Army Headquarters up to 1959 but the officers appointed were normally seconded to other duties considered more pressing at the time. It is alarming to think that even though our Defence Forces are barely over fifty years in existence many documents relevant to the period simply may not exist, or if they do exist, nobody knows exactly where.[4]

This short article remains prescient today. In it, Young identified the potential and importance of an archive in engendering morale and unit pride through the proper understanding that links to the past provide; the public relations benefits that a properly constituted archive would generate; and, most importantly, for the preservation of historical accuracy.

During 1980, Young was deployed on a six-month tour of duty as an Operations Staff Officer at UNIFIL (United Nations Interim Force in Lebanon) Headquarters, based at Naquora, in the south of the country. His former boss in the Press and Information Office, Vincent Savino, now a Colonel and the Senior Irish Officer (SIO) in theatre, described him as 'at all times a most efficient Staff Officer, who showed great dedication and professionalism and commendable initiative in dealing with situations which demanded tact and patience in their resolving.' His work also warranted a special commendation from Colonel J.C.A.J. de Vogel, the Chief Operations Officer in UNIFIL HQ, who described his conduct in carrying out his various duties as thorough and conscientious.

Upon his return to Ireland, Young was personally invited by the then UNIFIL Force Commander, the Irish Lieutenant General William 'Bull' Callaghan, to return to Lebanon for a further two years, in the highly prestigious role of Assistant Press Officer to Timur Goksel, the UNIFIL Press and Information Officer and Spokesman once described by Robert Fisk as 'perhaps the most powerful man in southern Lebanon.' This could well have been a high-flying military career in the making, possibly marking Young out as General Staff material at some time in the future. Such was Young's focus and dedication, however, that he turned the offer down as the first case for the establishment of the Archives was under consideration at that time.

Despite still being two years before it would be re-established, Young was more or less fully engaged with archives following his return from Lebanon in late-1980. In September of that year the Directorate of Planning and Research included the establishment of a Military Archives, with a strength of one commandant, two sergeants and one corporal, in their annual proposals.[5] The following year this was updated to include the proposed selection of the Magazine Fort in the Phoenix Park as a suitable location for the Military Archives. While the Magazine Fort was ultimately not selected as the location, the preparation for its re-establishment had been ongoing in the immediately preceding years, with microfilm readers, cameras, film, and archival boxes having been procured by the Defence Forces for that purpose.[6]

In August 1981, Young was promoted to the rank of Commandant. That same year, his commanding officer and Director of Intelligence, Colonel J. Egan, formally noted for the attention of the Chief of Staff that 'I strongly recommend that the appointment of archivist be activated and be appointed.' It seemed as if the stars were beginning to align for Young and the Military Archives when, as it had since the 1920s, it yet again fell short of receiving the necessary resourcing or being taken quite as seriously as it required to achieve its full potential.

In March of 1982, Young discovered that the Chief of Staff had proposed that the Military Archives be established on an *ad hoc* basis, something Young described as the 'one great fault' of the plan. While he was encouraged by the fact that the Archives were to be stood-up at all, he expressed his serious concerns in detail to the Director of Intelligence. They are worth presenting here in full given that, just as in O'Connell's letter of 24 August 1936, in this letter Young anticipated and foreshadowed the various problems and shortcomings that would afflict the Military Archives into the 2000s. To his great credit some of these had more effect than others, as he mitigated against many through a combination of sheer determination and force of personality. It would not be until 1998 that a review of the Defence Forces allocated one commandant, one captain and one sergeant to the official strength of the Military Archives.

One of the basic criteria on which an Archives works is that of trust. If people have material that is both valuable to themselves and to history, they will not release them to an office which has no sense of permanence and official recognition. They need to be reassured that their material will be properly looked after and not thrown into boxes after a few years and neglected as has happened in the past. I have experienced great difficulties in the past few years trying to persuade eminent ex-military personnel to donate their documentation and have failed to acquire anything of note as they are justifiably wary of the non-permanent aspect of an Archives.

From the point of view of the Defence Forces, it would be well-nigh impossible to impress on units the necessity for preserving files if there is no official recognition and proper establishment. Advice on future preservation of documents would tend to be ignored if it does not come from an official source.

Researchers using material from an *ad hoc* archives would experience great difficulty in pinning down correct references for their notes. Also reference to a semi-official archives would encourage many other researchers to avail of the facilities which obviously would be limited if the Archives was not permanent.

For an archives to be successful, it must be all-embracing, *i.e.* it must cover the whole period required and not just certain aspects. As it stands as present, there are many gaps in our records and these can only be filled by retired personnel and by documentation held by outside, non-military personnel. As I have already stated this material will not be forthcoming until such time that the Archives is recognised as official and permanent. If the Archives is established on an *ad hoc* basis, it will be extremely difficult to make the case in the future to give it permanent status so we will lose out in the long term while gaining in the short term.

If a staff is selected on an *ad hoc* basis they will have to be got from existing staffs. There is no guarantee that this staff will be permanent in that the sections from which they are drawn may look for them again after a period. Also any staff selected would need to have a sense of permanence if they are to work properly. Again on an *ad hoc* basis it would be very difficult to hand pick the personnel required as other sections would be unwilling, in many cases, to release the existing staff.[7]

1982–1983: MILITARY ARCHIVES – THE FIRST YEAR

Four months later, in July 1982, the Military Archives was re-established on a full-time basis following a twenty-three-year absence. The Archives was now based at the Red House, Army Headquarters, Parkgate, in Dublin. In October 1983, Young took to the pages of *An Cosantóir* magazine to introduce the Defence Forces and, to the extent of its circulation, the wider Irish public, to the re-established Military Archives.[8]

The first requirement was to tackle the neglect of the previous years. This started with the collected archival documents which had been stored at Cathal Brugha Barracks for safekeeping in the absence of a formal Military Archives establishment – the same documents that had been collected and organised since the 1920s, most notably by the likes of Colonel J.J. O'Connell, Lieutenant Colonel N.C. Harrington, and Commandant G.S. Cox. Harrington had in fact been instrumental in encouraging Young to advocate for the re-establishment of the Military Archives, and in 1983 Young wrote to Harrington's daughter, seeking assistance in the form of any useful documentation of his that she may have had in her possession.[9]

The main duties in re-establishing the Military Archives involved the collecting, arranging, and indexing of records, which by its nature was painstaking and meticulous. This was further complicated by the interest that the Military Archives had generated, with the number of queries being received having a detrimental effect on getting the records indexed. (This balancing act between meeting and servicing immediate public demand and cataloguing material for future release is one with which archivists will be extremely familiar!)

Young also faced the difficulty posed by the fact that most of the documents in his custody were closed to the public. In this regard, however, he correctly anticipated the issue being resolved by the proposed National Archives Bill which was due to come before Dáil Éireann and which would include the 'thirty-year rule.' This rule would obligate departments of state to make their official records over thirty years old available for public inspection at the National Archives, except in very specific circumstances.[10] The Act was published in 1986 and the Military Archives would become one of only a very few designated 'places of deposit' for state records, outside of the National Archives itself, under the terms of that Act in 1990.

During its first year of being re-established the Military Archives was receiving on average ten queries a week. Of these, Young proudly noted that all but two had been successfully answered, and that the two outstanding were of an extremely specific nature about which no records were available.

Young had realised the first step in his vision for the Military Archives – a vision succinctly expressed in his 1983 article's final paragraph:

> The purpose of any archives is to protect the past so as to understand the present and to plan for the future. A Military Archives is more important than most as by knowing our past history, we attain a greater sense of identity with an understanding of our own unit, and so improve morale and *esprit de corps* which are essential elements of military life.

Much like his predecessor J.J. O'Connell, Young threw himself wholly into his work and became a force within the wider realm of Defence Forces history, culture, and heritage. He regularly contributed articles and reviews to *An Cosantóir*, almost always including a reference to the Archives, its work, or the significance of its holdings to the subject under discussion. In the fiftieth anniversary special issue of *An Cosantóir* in September 1989, for example, Young published *The Way We Were,* an article examining the military aspects of the Emergency period. While a capable historian, he maintained an archivist's perspective, commenting in this article on the lack of historical information on the military aspects of this important period, largely attributed to the lack of archival legislation, with the Act only due to come in to force the following year. Young's literary contributions were not just there to fill column inches either. *The Way We Were* was awarded first place in that year's annual

Captain Seamus Kelly Memorial Awards. This award was presented for the most significant article published in *An Cosantóir* each year. Articles were judged on originality, professionalism (military and journalistic), interest, literary style, format and readability. Young's winning article beat off competition from authors including Robert Fisk and Ronan Fanning.

Young was made for the work and was really coming into his own, with a natural predilection for scholarly and intellectual pursuits. It brought him back in contact with his old comrade Robert Fisk, who was undertaking his PhD in Trinity College in the early 1980s. Fisk became a regular visitor to the Red House to view Defence records. He recalled Young taking him into 'an austere, cold but dry room, full of uncat-alogued Coast Watching Service files and other records,' with Young always making sure that there was hot coffee on hand. Of these earliest days of the re-established Military Archives, Fisk recalled how 'very little was open of any archives at the time, and in general it was a matter of persuasion' to gain the trust of state departments to get access to their records. This was, of course, typical of the times and not unique to Defence. Fisk had also been visiting Sherkin Island for research, talking to participants and relatives of the Coast Watching Service. He fondly recalled how 'Peter gave me carte blanche to look at the coast watching material, once he'd reviewed it first of course.'

Fisk completed his PhD in 1983, with his dissertation being published as his ground-breaking book *In Time of War*. To Fisk, Young was a kin-dred spirit, recalling that:

Peter constantly talked about the Civil War, he lived in the twenties in many ways. He was someone who was a bit of a student who in different circumstances may well have left the army and been a scholar.

It is important to note that not everyone within the Defence Forces fully appreciated the national significance of what Young had initiated. This should be no surprise, as earlier chapters have described how attitudes ranging from a lack of appreciation to outright hostility from certain individuals in key positions had traditionally been one of the greatest threats to the survival of the Military Archives. This did not change during its twenty-three-year hiatus. Young experienced just how significant this could be in 1984, when an officer of no lesser position than the Chief of Staff himself, Lieutenant General Gerald O'Sullivan, decided to take it upon himself to transfer Young to the 5th Infantry Battalion as one of his final edicts before retiring. This, he informed Young, was for the good of his career, as remaining too long in one appointment was not considered a positive thing for an officer's promotion prospects, even though it would have meant the effective closing down of the Military Archives. Fortunately, the incoming Chief of Staff, Lieutenant General Tadgh O'Neill, saw sense and asked Young to remain at his post until a successor could be trained. Thankfully, Young was never forced to move on. The view that a posting to the Military Archives was to be considered as something potentially detrimental to an officer's promotion prospects would linger almost until the present, however, with some officers serving at the Archives even receiving formal notice that pursuing such an appointment could be considered as such. Nor would this be the last attempt to undermine the position of the Military Archives, as will be discussed later in this and in the following chapter.

MUSEUM CONNECTIONS

Young recognised that the Defence Forces, like any other national organisation, had an obligation to preserve its past for posterity. He was also outspoken and forthright in his opinion that the organisation had been guilty of neglect in this regard and had already lost much of the military material that was used in the sixty years between the establishment of the National Army and the re-establishment of the Military Archives. Peter viewed the re-establishment of the Archives as a step towards addressing this situation and the establishment of a military museum as a necessary parallel step in this process. Like the Archives, the matter of military museums had its own long and drawn-out history. In 1982, the Military Archives and military museums fell very much within the same milieu, with Peter firmly at the centre. It is not possible to properly discuss the Military Archives at this time without referring to military museums.

The first serious suggestions of a military museum occurred as far back as 1950, following the receipt of the Irish Government of the Bodkin Report on the Arts in Ireland. [11] It had been proposed that a joint military / civilian committee be established to examine the issue, and to this end the Chief of Staff appointed Colonel Dan Bryan and Lieutenant Colonel Whelan of Intelligence Branch to the task. Unfortunately, it came to naught after the Minister for Defence ruled to 'defer further action.'[12]

In 1973, the Assistant Chief of Staff raised the matter again and drew up a policy document identifying three types of potential military museums for consideration. The first was a *National Military Museum*, encompassing all material of a military nature related to the national military effort of any period. The second, an *Army Museum*, focusing solely on the Irish Army since its foundation to the exclusion of any other military material. The third, *a Military Museum*, was the most diluted version and one which would house all material with any military significance. The Assistant Chief of Staff formed the opinion that a *National Military Museum* would be the most appropriate course of action and the one most appealing to the public.

A memorandum on the matter was sent to the Department of Education and to the National Museum. The Director of the National Museum at that time, A.T. Lucas, was totally opposed, expressing the opinion that the National Museum already fulfilled the role of a National Military Museum, and that the idea was too ambitious. Lucas suggested that a Defence Forces Museum was the only viable option, and that even to achieve this, the Defence Forces would have to be able to staff it on a full-time basis with professionally trained personnel. Just as in 1950, this project again came to nothing. Lucas, it must be acknowledged, had a valid argument, commenting that:

I am, to some extent, acquainted with the Military Museum at the Curragh and its history. That history reflects the fundamental problem that besets all institutions of this nature: lack of continuity resulting from the absence of permanent personnel whose sole duty is the maintenance of the museum. In the absence of such personnel, the history of an institution is one of alternating activity and stagnation, corresponding to the enthusiasm of the persons in temporary charge of it.[13]

It was another five years before the matter was properly addressed again. On 7 September 1978 a new 'Steering Committee on the Establishment of a Museum of a Military Nature' met for the first time in the Conference Room of the Department of Defence, Parkgate, Dublin. The purpose of this committee was to guide a military analyst – Commandant P. McMenamin – who was appointed to study the matter of the establishment of a military museum. The committee consisted of representatives from the National Museum of Ireland, the Department of Defence, and the Defence Forces. The terms of reference of the committee were to examine the format of such a museum, the extent and nature of its exhibits, the costs of building a new premises or adapting an existing one, and the necessary structure, organisation and annual running costs.[14]

The Defence Forces was keen and pro-active. A comprehensive survey of potentially suitable museum material in its custody was directed and completed by May 1980. However, things were not working out auspiciously within the wider political sphere. By 1982, the preparation of a national policy on the development of the museum services, first announced by the Department of Education on 15 September 1981, was no longer being pursued due to lack of finance and ongoing considerations about who exactly held responsibility for museum services in Ireland.

In June 1982, a month before he would officially take the helm of a re-established Military Archives, Peter Young met in Army Headquarters with the Quartermaster-General (Major General John Gallagher) and a Senior Staff Officer from Barrack Services Section (Commandant J. Moriarty). The National Museum of Ireland was represented by Oliver

Snoddy. Also in attendance were Mary McGrath and Frank Harte, who in 1975 had been contracted to draft the plan to convert the Magazine Fort in the Phoenix Park into a military museum.

This meeting was called to consider the possibility of the newly re-established Military Archives being based at the Magazine Fort, with a view to the site eventually also incorporating a military museum. Harte, the architect, advised against this for practical reasons. Fitting out shelving for the Archives would lead to needless expense when they would eventually have to be removed again so that the bays could be levelled in order to develop the museum complex. Instead, he recommended working in reverse – finding an interim location for the Military Archives and initiating a new study of the Magazine Fort with a view to developing a military museum which would then incorporate the Military Archives. This study, he suggested, would be carried out by a board consisting of members of the Defence Forces, Department of Defence, and National Museum of Ireland, as the three primary potential contributors of artefacts and exhibits.[15]

In September, Young and Harte inspected the Magazine Fort and both reported to the Quartermaster-General that the site was nothing short of excellent. The proposed development was for a single-floor facility with three main functions. The first functional area would consist of accommodation for administrative staff, a library and an archive. This section would be equipped with a researcher reading room and audiovisual facilities. The second area was to be a 150–200 person capacity auditorium for lectures and conferences, also boasting modern audiovisual equipment and a coffee bar for serving light refreshments. The third section would take the form of four separate galleries to fulfil the museum function. The layout of the Magazine Fort and immediately surrounding land was identified as very suitable to display larger items such as tanks or heavy weapons.

The plan was ambitious and impressive. Harte envisioned a single-story building with fourteen-foot ceilings throughout and as few intermediate supports as possible, maximising the flexibility of the layout. The 23,722 square feet of floor-space was to be concrete finished with ceramic tiles. The walls were to be primarily glass, with solid walls only where engineering required. The estimated cost of this project was £830,270 – well over €2,000,000 in modern money.[16]

In November, Young met at Army Headquarters with the Quartermaster-General, the Officer-in-Charge of Barrack Services (Lieutenant Colonel Begley) and Commandant McMenamin, the officer who had been first tasked with the museum feasibility study. At this meeting it was decided that the prospective museum being pursued should be limited to Defence Forces military history, with a view to expanding to wider Irish military history in the future should funding arise.

Regarding the all-important funding, the Quartermaster-General informed the meeting that, unfortunately, there would be no money available in 1983 and that *some* money would *potentially* become available in 1984 and afterwards, on an annual basis, until the project was completed. While disappointing, this did not dampen their resolve.

A letter was prepared for the attention of the Chief of Staff, to be submitted through the Director of Intelligence, recommending the formation of a committee to prepare in detail for the eventual opening of a military museum. This committee would initially consist of only military personnel until their initial investigations were completed. The committee would focus on establishing the basic principles for developing the museum, investigating the suitable equipment and resources, deciding how and where this material would be stored in the interim, investigating the feasibility of regional and local military museums, and to generally coordinate all work within the Defence Forces of a historical nature.[17]

This committee was duly established by the Chief of Staff and directed to investigate the possibility of a military museum at the Magazine Fort. The members met for the first time on 10 May 1983 and were based out of the Military Archives, then still located in the Red House. The committee consisted of Lieutenant Colonel Con Costello (Chairman) and Commandants Young, Betson and Lynch – representatives of the branches of the Chief of Staff, Adjutant General and Quartermaster General.[18]

Captain D. McGonnell was subsequently appointed by the Director of Engineering at the request of Costello, who for obvious reasons wanted an engineer on the committee. The previously drafted 1980 inventory was circulated to all corps and formations to be checked and updated, and support and willingness to provide museum items was widely received.

The committee set to work visiting locations throughout the country, with particular interest in the various coastal defence positions and their artillery pieces, at places like Fort Mitchell and Fort Dunree. At the same time, Costello was networking and reaching out for advice and assistance to curators and conservators in many of Ireland's main cultural institutions and service providers.

By the end of 1984, however, things were starting to flounder yet again, with the Minister for Defence announcing in 1985 that:

> In light of current financial restrictions and having regard to the view of the Director of the National Museum on the need for 'a totally professional approach to the establishment, organisation and development of such a museum' it is most unlikely that a military museum will be established in the foreseeable future.[19]

This was a blow to Young's plans. No purpose-built military museum in the Magazine Fort meant no purpose-built Military Archives in the Magazine Fort either. While extremely disappointing, it was not the end of the matter. With customary military stoicism, the Chief of Staff proceeded to establish yet another committee, this time tasked with coordinating the work of local / barrack museums throughout the Defence Forces, with Peter naturally remaining as the lynchpin of it all.

THE NATIONAL ARCHIVES OF IRELAND ACT, 1986

The Military Archives quickly gained momentum during the early 1980s. Valuable records were deposited from various sources, including the papers of 'Squad' member Colonel Joe Leonard, and those of George Walsh, a founding member of the Irish Volunteers, which as mentioned in the previous chapter had been transferred to the Bureau of Military History several decades before. Historical artefacts also started to arrive at Young's door, including a 'Blue Hussars' tunic and various items of vintage dress uniform, including that of Colonel Dan Bryan. The Military Archives was soon fully functional, operating and serving the public five days a week. As the Archives were slowly but surely professionalising and beginning to receive their due attention within the Defence Forces, the same was happening outside.

On 23 September 1985, a briefing session was held in the Institute of Public Administration on the implications of the new National Archives Bill, which was before the Dáil at that time. The Defence Forces was a scheduled body under that Bill and would consequently be affected by its legislation. Therefore, it was deemed essential that Peter Young attend, and the £75 attendance fee was duly paid by the Directorate of Training.

In 1986, the National Archives of Ireland Act was published. Consolidating the functions of the State Papers Office (SPO) and Public Records Office (PRO) this was the first piece of legislation relating to archival records published by the Irish state in its sixty-eight years of existence. Even more significantly, for the first time it provided in law for the public right of access to state records.

The Act focused the attention of the Defence Forces and the Department of Defence on the requirements of the Military Archives. Against the background of these impending statutory obligations, the Military Archives was found lacking, though certainly not through Young's doing. It was still based out of the sub-standard accommodation of the Red House, staffed only on an *ad hoc* basis by Young, his deputy Captain Victor Laing, Sergeant Joe White and Private Brendan Mahoney.

The fact that Young did not have an official appointment of 'Officer-in-Charge, Military Archives' to occupy led to difficulties akin to a game of administrative musical chairs. As there was no official appointment for Young to occupy, he had been posted on paper as the Commander of Headquarters Company of the 5th Infantry Battalion and then attached to the Chief of Staff's Branch. This was in order to vacate the Commandant's appointment he had previously filled in Intelligence Section so it would not be left short a senior staff officer, but also meant that Young was blocking a Commandant's appointment in the 5th Infantry Battalion. A captain from Intelligence Section was promoted to Commandant and took over Young's vacancy, leaving Intelligence with a Captain's vacancy. The Director of Intelligence considered the various courses of action available to him (including returning Young to Intelligence Section and leaving the newly promoted Commandant surplus to establishment) and recommended to the Chief of Staff that Young continue to block 'an appropriate appointment' (i.e., in the 5th Battalion as opposed to Intelligence) and be attached to the Chief of Staff's Branch as an archivist. In the meantime, application would be made for the adjustment of the Defence Forces Establishment to be revised and to provide for the staffing of the Military Archives. Concurrently, another officer would be identified to undertake the Diploma in Archives Studies at UCD with a view to establishing a successor to Young, deemed more important now that the National Archives Act was coming into force, bringing with it increased accountability for the Defence Forces should state records suffer neglect.

The Director of Intelligence identified three shortlisted nominees who were interested and suitable to undertake archivist training in UCD and subsequent employment as archivists – Captain Sean Hamill, Captain John Sheehan and the aforementioned Captain Victor Laing. Of these, it was Laing who proved successful. He had, in fact, been negotiating a move to the Military Archives since 1983. Laing was promoted to Captain in 1985, deployed to Lebanon with the Army in the winter of 1985/86 and was posted into the Staff Officer position at the Military Archives upon his return. He undertook the Junior Command and Staff Course in 1986/87 and then undertook the Diploma in Archives course in UCD 1987–1988.

Upon Laing's return from college, the Military Archives had moved across the city, from the Red House to Cathal Brugha Barracks. The move was not perfect; Laing recalled that the former St Patrick's Hall, which was the main archival repository until 2016, initially had to serve as both offices and reading room due to several structural issues with the main building. Still, these issues were eventually remedied, and overall it was an improvement on the previous accommodation.

Meanwhile Young had been posted to the Military College since October 1989 to undertake the Command and Staff Course, during which time Laing was acting Officer-in-Charge of the Military Archives. Unsurprisingly, the College Commandant of the Command and Staff School noted that Young displayed a special aptitude for 'military history and the history of the Defence Forces.' Throughout this course, he displayed the same high standards and competency as an Army Officer that had marked him out for the offer of a special posting as Assistant Press Officer to Timur Goksel almost a decade before:

> Comdt Young was an excellent student. As Class President his positive influence contributed immensely to the success of the course. A well-rounded individual and a man of independent thought, he was never afraid to put his well-reasoned views on the line. His attitude towards the course, initiative displayed and general contributions were very good. His judgement and decisiveness were very good. When placed in positions of responsibility and control he had a very good influence upon those with whom he worked and an ability to achieve results.[20]

YOUNG'S CONCERNS: STAFFING AND ACCOMMODATION CONCERNS

Just two weeks after his return to the Archives, Young wrote to the Director of Intelligence to bring to his attention matters that 'deserve action sooner rather than later.'[21] The first was the matter of the formal establishment of the Military Archives. The fact that the Military Archives had not been *officially* established as part of the Defence Forces structure meant that staff had no security of tenure. Young had no administrative responsibility for them and those to whom they did answer had no interest in them as they did not get any work out of them for their own units or sections. As a result, his staff were missing out on courses, selection for overseas service and many other similar aspects of the rhythm of military life. From a very practical perspective, not having an official establishment meant that the Military Archives could not formally requisition equipment within the Army logistical system. This covered practically everything from furniture to stationery and from telephones to cleaning equipment.

Retaining and expanding its current accommodation was also a concern. A decision had been made by government in 1988 to close Collins Barracks, in the Arbor Hill area of Dublin, as a military installation. With the impending posting of additional troops to Cathal Brugha Barracks (among other locations), Young was concerned that, as the Military Archives was not on the official establishment, it stood to lose real estate in favour of operational units. Conversely, the concept of the Military Archives being accommodated at Collins Barracks following its closure had been raised in the Dáil just a few months earlier. Deputy Eric J. Byrne, of the Labour Party, asked the Fianna Fáil Minister for Defence, Deputy Brian Lenihan, if he could consider 'the establishment of a military history museum and archive centre in Collins Barracks, Dublin 8, when it is no longer required for military purposes'[22] while Deputy Ruairi Quinn, also Labour, asked if he would, 'in conjunction with the Department of Finance and Dublin Corporation, ensure that the terms of sale include a requirement upon the purchasers to provide for a military museum.' Lenihan's answer was non-committal and offered no solace to Young and his concerns about the government's commitment to the future accommodation of the Military Archives. Lenihan informed the House that it was intended that Collins Barracks would be offered for sale when the military units located there had relocated, and that the imposition by the Department of Defence on the purchaser of the barracks of any conditions regarding the future use of the property would not be legally enforceable. Quinn's response was characteristically eloquent and precise:

> Will the Minister not agree that this country could do with the benefit of a military museum that is accessible to the general public, that Collins Barracks is perhaps unique in Europe in that it has been continuously occupied for military purposes since it was constructed, that, it is the oldest set of buildings so used and, that a vendor can set pretty much whatever legal conditions on the sale of property he chooses and the legal advice the Minister has quoted is patent nonsense?

Not having a formal establishment was also having an impact on the public image of the Military Archives. While Young was relatively successful in acquiring private donations, there were still other potential donors who had expressed their reluctance to donate material until there existed a formal establishment.

Young also expressed a clear concern in relation to the attitude of the Department of Defence to the Military Archives. Describing the Department's attitude as 'unclear at present', having an official establishment, he told the Director of Intelligence, would 'strengthen our defences against any efforts that might be made to undermine our position.' And attempt to undermine them they did.

YOUNG'S CONCERNS: MILITARY ARCHIVES V DEPARTMENT OF DEFENCE

Young's second area of serious concern elaborated on this point and was one he described in his letter under the heading of 'Military Archives v Department of Defence.' Examples of both the passive and deliberate mismanagement of historical records, particularly those of a military nature, had been a recurring feature of the Irish state's relationship to archives and has been mentioned in earlier chapters: the burning of records by Dublin Castle staff following the signing of the Truce in 1921; the destruction of the Public Records Office during the Civil War; the wholesale handover of intelligence records from Military Intelligence to the Garda Síochána in 1926 (current location unknown); the 1932 'Burn Order'; and the failure of the State to enact any archival legislation until sixty-four years after its foundation. Young's concerns in this letter described a situation which suggested a similar trend towards the neglect of records, in this case by the Department of Defence. Exacerbating the situation, the Department of Defence was now seeking the return of Departmental records from the Military Archives, to be located, not even at the National Archives but at a proposed departmental archive. Following years of neglect, once the government's intention to publish a National Archives Act was announced and having seen the momentum of the Military Archives, the Department of Defence started to make a play to have a separate archive of their own. Young wrote:

Since 1976, I have been collecting archival material, mainly military in origin but also including two collections that originated in the Department of Defence. These are:-

(a) "A" Files 1922–1925: These files are largely military in nature. They were rescued from destruction in the late 1970s the day before they were due to be collected for disposal. The Department has never expressed an interest in them heretofore. They are of great historical value and we have made extensive use of them in the past and regard them as an integral part of our Civil War files.

(b) Departmental "2/Bar" Files 1925-1946: Again these files were dumped in an old block hut that was situated inside Planning and Research Section in DFHQ. We spent approximately 18 months sorting through every single file, extracting those of archival value. The remainder where then destroyed. It is possible that all of them would have been destroyed if we had not checked them. The vast majority of the files are again military in nature and are hardly of use to the Department at this stage. We make extensive use of them and again regard them as an integral part of our archives.

It would be fruitless handing over these collections to a Departmental archives as they are military and historical. We have acquired knowledge and expertise over the years and to hand over these files to someone who would have neither would not make sense.

A STATUTORY PLACE OF DEPOSIT

Less than four months after Young wrote this letter, on 21 December 1990, the Taoiseach, Charles J. Haughey, approved the deposit of the records of the Defence Forces, Department of Defence and Army Pensions Board at the Military Archives. This manoeuvre was played by Laing, who had made representations for the designation and overseen its progress during Young's absence on the Command and Staff Course. The Military Archives was now an official 'place of deposit' under the terms provided for in Section 13 of the National Archives Act, strengthening the Archives' position and bolstering its defences against interference through the conferring upon it of statutory rights and obligations. The other nominated places of deposit under the terms of the Act were the Geological Survey of Ireland, the National Library of Ireland and the National Museum of Ireland. The main difference with the Military Archives, however, was that it was now the legally designated repository for all of the records of its parent Department of State, and the valuable 'A/' and '2/' files, with which Young was so concerned, remained in its custody. It was not, however, the last time that the Department of Defence would try to undermine the Military Archives.

In just eight years, Young had brought the Military Archives from non-existent to a nationally significant, statutorily mandated, archival institution. Despite a long way still to go, the Military Archives faced into the new decade with confidence.

Chapter 6

1991–1999: THE COMMANDANT PETER YOUNG YEARS (PART 2)

A s the re-established Military Archives entered its second decade it was not only a research facility but a flagship for Defence Forces public relations. One researcher for example, a retired US Army officer and veteran of the Second World War and Korea, was sufficiently impressed that he was moved to write to the Chief of Staff about his research visit to the Military Archives:

> Here I had the good fortune to meet Commandant Peter Young and Sergeant Joe White. Both of these fine men were invaluable in helping me with my research. Their kindness and courtesy, plus a damn fine cup of tea, reflected the highest standards of the Army Archives in particular and the Irish Army in general.[1]

Dr Pat McCarthy, of the Military History Society of Ireland, similarly recalled in interview his positive experiences at the Military Archives during this time.

> First of all, the great tradition of a wonderful, welcoming, helpful staff, was in a sense established by Peter. That was the criteria – wonderful, welcom-

ing, helpful. They just couldn't do enough for you. And I thought the little reading room, which could accommodate three at a push, two normally, was great…One thing that impressed me was that, I'm not a historian, but he made me as welcome as if I was a professor of history. Didn't matter. Everybody was welcome there, and that was typical of the man.[2]

In early 1991, Young invited Mr Justice Niall McCarthy, in his capacity as the Chairman of the National Archives Advisory Council, to visit the Military Archives. The Council had been established in January of 1987 in order to advise the Minister with responsibility for the National Archives (the Minister for Culture, Heritage and the Gaeltacht) in the exercise of their powers under the National Archives Act and on all matters affecting archives and their public use. This visit was of considerable benefit to the institution, raising both its status and the morale of Young and his team. McCarthy found it 'a most rewarding visit' and commented on the professionalism with which Young and his staff were looking after the records in their custody. He also remarked, however, that they were 'working under significant restraints of expenditure and staff.' Following his visit, McCarthy wrote to the Minister for Defence, raising the pressing requirements for staff, accommodation and computers. He specifically noted Young's 'enthusiasm and professionalism' and that there was 'no impression of any failure to make the maximum use of minimum facilities' on his part. In his letter, McCarthy said that:

> I write to request your personal interest in a feature of the Defence Forces which is of growing importance in promoting goodwill, interest and a better understanding of the role of the Defence Forces to the general public. Indeed, it was with considerable pride that I saw the extent and quality of the archives at Cathal Brugha Barracks; one would like to see that pride shared by all.[3]

Given the natural order of things within the military and the civil service, the Minister then wrote to the Chief of Staff for input into his reply, and the Chief of Staff wrote to the Director of Intelligence. The Acting Director – at that time Lieutenant Colonel John Duggan – provided four observations:

a. At present, there is no formally established staff for Archives work – existing staff are on loan from areas already overworked.

b. A case has been made for properly established staff and this is being considered in conjunction with the overall review of Defence Force staffing.

c. Accommodation is an ongoing problem – particularly in view of the proposed rationalisation plans which include the sale of some military establishments. However plans are in hand to supplement existing accommodation.

d. Equipment, particularly computers and an archive programme, are accepted as essential equipment. This will be dealt with in long-term planning but no immediate solution is available.[4]

Further to this, Duggan noted that the competing demands on Defence Forces staff and budgets had to be stressed, and that the needs of the Military Archives needed to be balanced against many others within the organisation. Interestingly, the four points raised by Duggan were matters over which the Department of Defence and the Minister had more control than the Chief of Staff.

'INFORMATION...INFORMATION...'

Along with Young, White, Laing and Mahoney, the Military Archives had the benefit of the voluntary services of Denis McCarthy. McCarthy's initial contact with the Defence Forces came through his enthusiasm for armoured vehicles, writing a series of articles in collaboration with Adrian J. English and Peter Leslie on the subject for *An Cosantóir* magazine in the 1970s. In his professional life, McCarthy was a Vocational Teacher in Liberties College, Dublin, who taught computers when they were still in their infancy. Having heard about the re-establishment of the Military Archives, McCarthy saw the opportunity to combine both of these passions while contributing to its work. As he described it in his own wryly humorous and entertaining writing style,

> Vague rumours about an elusive Military Archives began to take concrete form, and it transpired that once upon a time such a body had come briefly into existence, and was in the process of slowly being resuscitated. The Army even acquired a qualified Archivist and probably by mistake, appointed him to the Archives. With a total staff of one sergeant, there seemed an opportunity for a pushy, arrogant, ruthless thick-skinned civilian to worm his way in amongst the records, with a little bit of luck and a lot of guile. It worked – and soon spare time started to be spent in a dilapidated building burrowing through mouldering files, rejoicing at the discovery of letters which said 'see enclosed drawings' and less joyfully discovering that the 'enclosed drawings' weren't.[5]

The matter of the computerisation of the Military Archives was a significant challenge for Young, as something over which he had no direct control within the Army structure. Having McCarthy's support as a civilian expert and advocate meant that there was someone in a position to make representations outside of the military chain-of-command that were closed to Young as a serving officer. As of 1990, the Department of Defence had not identified the Military Archives as a priority for computerisation under its IT plan. McCarthy had prepared a memorandum on the suggested necessary equipment, but this did not conform to the standard laid down by the Defence Forces' Director of Planning and Research, meaning that even if funding had been available, the proposed model would have meant that technical support and maintenance would have proved difficult. The National Archives had recently commissioned a feasibility study to examine computerisation by the Central Computing Service[6] and it had proved too expensive for them too. However, the National Archives were still working with an interim measure of four PCs, while the Military Archives only had the loan of McCarthy's Atari 520 ST (for which he had gone to the effort of writing bespoke cataloguing software).

Young recommended to the Director of Intelligence (at that time Colonel James 'Jimmy' Flynn – later Brigadier General and a consummate friend to the Military Archives right until his death in 2021) that a request be made to the Director of Planning and Research for a feasibility study to be carried out to identify and formalise the requirement for computerisation. Once the requirements were properly established, Young recommended that external funding would need to be sought, estimating that the cost would likely be in the region of £15,000.[7]

In the meantime, McCarthy exercised his freedom as a civilian and citizen to address the matter more directly, raising the issue with the Minister for Defence regularly and candidly between 1990 and 1994. The opening salvo went as follows:

Dear Minister.

Thank you for your courteous reception of my admittedly ill-mannered approach at the opening of the 'EX-CAMERA' exhibition at the National Library on Thursday 10th May. I appreciate the demands on your time and the pressures of your position will limit the attention you may give to pushy members of the public, and will take this opportunity to restate briefly my proposals.

Having spent a considerable number of years researching Irish Army armoured vehicles I have been fortunate enough to develop an excellent working relationship with the Military Archives and would like to see its status and resources improve. To this end, I have been trying to bully them into considering an innovative application of computers (see article 'Information, Information' enclosed). While willing, the Archives has

been handicapped by the lack of an official establishment and the conse-
quent lack of resources – i.e., no computers...[8]

The reply from the Minster for Defence (Brian Lenihan) came in July
of that year, informing McCarthy that the funds were unfortunately
not available. However, the Minister visited the Military Archives on
26 April 1991 to survey the situation for himself, and recommended
that, in the absence of Departmental monies, a case should be made for
National Lottery funds. No less determined, McCarthy continued to
pursue the matter in parallel through correspondence. His letter dated
10 August 1993 to Minister David Andrews of Fianna Fáil, who then held
the Defence portfolio, went as follows:

Dear Minister.
My yearly letter to determine whether there is *life as we know it* in the
Department of Defence. I also have this naïve hope that as a constituent
of yours I may perhaps get somewhat further than just a mere citizen.

Specifically, this deals (still) with the prospect of using computers in
the Military Archives. This correspondence was initiated in July 1990,
requesting a policy decision – i.e. no immediate expenditure – that computers should if possible be used from the outset in the setting up of the
Military Archives. I am aware that the matter is 'under consideration'
having been informed of this in January 1991, December 1991, January
1992 and February 1992.

The matter is now largely academic, as the Military Archives now
have the use of two computers [one of which was McCarthy's personal
property] together with specialist software, and are making a fair effort at
trying to build up a computerised database of their holdings within their
limited resources, but I would appreciate the courtesy of a reply to the
points raised more than three years ago.[9]

The two-pronged approach of Young and McCarthy bore some fruit –
either through moral argument or attrition.[10] In August 1994, Minister

Andrews wrote to McCarthy to confirm that two personal computers, a server, a printer, a Local Area Network and database software, were due to be delivered to the Archives the following month. IT support would be provided by Defence Forces IT section and training provided to the Archives' staff. Like all its victories since 1924 this one was hard fought, but the Military Archives was slowly entering the information age.

GAINING MOMENTUM

Taking full ownership of his work, being the Archive Director was not merely a job but a vocation for Peter Young. So naturally, as the reputation of the Military Archives grew, so did his own. In 1992, the Director of Intelligence commented very favourably on the work of both Young and Laing, in relation to a three-day seminar in collaboration with the Military History Society of Ireland on the subject of the Emergency:

> I wish to compliment you and Capt Laing on the success of the recent Seminar on the Emergency. The concept was imaginative and the pro-gramme was most interesting if only for the mixture of 'Young Turks' alternating with the goodly smattering of old soldiers – many of whom had served the country so well during those difficult years. It was time that the period was remembered and that it was done with such fitting dignity and efficient organisation reflects credit on the Defence Forces and on you and your team for your hard work.[11]

The Military Archives developed what is known in military terminology as a 'habitual association' with the Military History Society of Ireland. Again, this was very much down to Peter and the historical conferences received great acclaim. Pat McCarthy recalled:

> I joined the Military History Society in 1986, and about a year or so later I was asked to join its Council. That's where I came in con-

tact with Peter. And I have to say from the beginning I was hugely, hugely impressed by him. Almost single handed he pushed the idea of conferences, and he organised them. He started off with one on the Emergency, which I think was our first one in 1992. He followed that with one on the Irish Defence Forces in the United Nations, which happened in 1995, and then one on – quite an adventurous topic in some sense – the Civil War. To mark the 75th anniversary of the Civil War we had one in 1997.

Peter, through his contacts, assembled for those, particularly for the UN one, you could say, a comprehensive panel of speakers. The Chief of Staff opened it, Liam Cosgrave – then Taoiseach – spoke at it, Noel Dorr spoke, Conor Cruise O'Brien, Robert Fisk on the Irish in UNIFIL, retired General Sean Mac Eoin… it really was a very comprehensive range of speakers. The same way when we did the Civil War one. He had guys speaking about the involvement of the Royal Navy and so on. As I say, Peter struck me as a guy who came up with an idea, and then went and delivered on it. They were absolutely super conferences.[12]

1992 was also the year that UCD offered Young the opportunity to pursue a PhD. As Young had no master's degree this was a singular honour and a reflection on the esteem in which he was held. The subject of his proposed thesis was to be *The Defence Forces during the Emergency*, the military aspects of which had been generally ignored by contemporary historians, who had commonly chosen to concentrate on the diplomatic, economic and political aspects of the Irish experience of the Second World War. The previously mentioned seminar had illustrated for Young the gap that existed at that time, between the fact and fiction of the war years in Irish historical memory. The PhD was to have been supervised by Ronan Fanning, the eminent Professor of Modern History and, while it would not require lectures or college attendance, it would involve considerable research in both Ireland and the UK. Unfortunately, this would have cost £1,200–£1,400 per year for tuition, guidance and the use of university facilities.

This was an opportunity that was too good to miss, and the completed work would have been of permanent value to the Defence Forces and to Irish historical enquiry in general. Young made application to the Director of Training for funding, and while the Director of Intelligence supported the case, the funding was not forthcoming, and an important opportunity was missed.

THE COLLINS BARRACKS SITE

In 1994, the matter of the relocation of the Military Archives arose again. This time the proposed location was Collins Barracks, Dublin. Collins Barracks was earmarked for closure in 1988 and in 1997 the Army would march out for the final time. This new plan would co-locate the Military Archives with the new National Museum of Ireland (NMI) venue – a £35 million investment in which one of the central attractions would be a dedicated military wing. The finer points of whether this would fall under the auspices of the Defence Forces or the NNI were still to be decided. Up until that point, an estimated 90% of the NMI's exhibits could not be put on display due to a lack of space, so it was desperately needed. At the same time, however, the Military Archives was also crying out for room to expand.

Young calculated that the Military Archives required 21,000 linear feet of shelving space and proposed a fit-for-purpose but realistic establishment, consisting of a reception area, twelve-seater reading room, lecture / exhibition hall and office / staff accommodation. This would, of course, raise the profile of the Military Archives and require a corresponding staff increase. The holdings of the Military Archives at that time were spread across three locations: 5,000 linear feet of archival boxes stored at the main St Patrick's Hall repository in Cathal Brugha Barracks; 4,500 linear feet of pensions and medal files (which would later become part of the *Military Service (1916–1923) Pensions Collection*) in 'Q' House, Cathal Brugha Barracks; and 2,500 still stored in the Red House. This accounted for only 12,000 linear feet. Young anticipated an additional 5,000 in the form of personnel files and other future accessions, and presciently, 1,000 linear feet to accommodate the records of the *Bureau of Military History* when they were eventually released for public inspection.[13]

In a meeting held in McKee Barracks on 31 May 1994, Dr Pat Wallace, the Director of the National Museum, confirmed that the Military Archives would be accommodated at the Collins Barracks site. This was part of the wider plans to incorporate a Defence Forces section at the museum and was considered a unique opportunity to ensure the preservation of the heritage and culture of the organisation. While the general shape of things was agreed upon, there were finer points to be teased out. The board had to determine how exactly the Defence Forces would be incorporated into the concept of the museum's initial development, entitled 'Historic Ireland.'[14] In relation to this, Captain Dan Harvey, himself now a well-known historian and author, wrote and presented a detailed submission covering both proposed themes and staffing.

The plans continued throughout 1995 and 1996, but while the museum element took precedence, the Military Archives became more and more of an afterthought. This was despite the fact that twice during 1995, two subsequent Fine Gael Minsters for Defence (Hugh Coveney and Seán Barrett) stated in the Dáil that there would be a Defence Forces section in the National Museum complex at Collins Barracks and that the Military Archives would be located there.[15] The minutes of the 17 of October 1996 meeting of the Collins Barracks Development Steering Group recorded that the proposal to co-locate the Archives had been forwarded to the Minister for Defence (Barrett) for approval. The minutes of 31 October and 29 November recorded that 'there have been no further developments since the last meeting of the group' in relation to the Military Archives. It did not help matters that direction came from government in late-1996 that the budget for the Collins Barracks project had to be cut by over £500,000.

By 1997, it was clear that the museum's military section could not be staffed by the Defence Forces and, while there would be collaboration and close contact with the Defence Forces, this section would fall under the remit of the National Museum of Ireland. At a meeting attended in January 1997 by representatives of the National Museum, the Defence Forces, and museum consultants Mr H. Sears and Ms C. Tanner, it was recorded that:

> The principle of locating Military Archives within Collins Barracks was accepted. This will be separately financed and the matter is currently being pursued. Staffing of the Archives will continue to be the responsibility of the Defence Forces. The consultants will hold discussions with the Military Archivist to determine the current and future needs to develop appropriate space.[16]

Senator Maurice Manning spoke strongly in support of the Military Archives and its relocation to the Museum complex at Collins Barracks in the context of a motion to the Seanad in 1999 concerning the National Archives and National Library.

> We have seen also the development of the Military Archive. Commandant Peter Young deserves enormous credit for what he has done there. It is proposed to move the Military Archive to Collins Barracks and, given the Army's long association with that barracks, it would be a very fitting place for it. I would ask the Minister, however, not to try to convert part of an old building into an archive. It will be cheaper in the long run to have a custom-built building. Given the technical problems of adaptation and all that could go wrong, it is false economy to try to rig out an old building rather than using the best technology available and starting from scratch.[17]

Not dissimilar to how the requests by the Chief of Staff to the Minister for Defence to officially establish the Military Archives during the 1920s were continually pushed further and further down the line to effectively say no by saying nothing, having the proposal for the move of the Military Archives to Collins Barracks 'with the Minster for consideration' meant that it would end up dragging on into the middle of the following decade.

THE MILITARY ARCHIVES GROWS

Despite various setbacks, the Military Archives came into its own during the 1990s under Young's guidance. Between 1992 and 1999 the Military Archives had on average 825 researchers a year and roughly similar numbers of postal or telephone queries. It was only in 1998, however, that a staff of one commandant, one captain and one sergeant was formalised in Defence Forces Administrative Instruction CS4, following the Defence Forces Review Implementation Plan of 1996. Young's monthly reports record that the Archives' queries and researchers not only originated in Ireland but came from as far afield as the UK, Germany, France, the Netherlands, the former Yugoslavia, Finland, the Middle East, USA, Canada, Australia, New Zealand, and Cambodia.

Outreach activities were also a core function of the Military Archives. Both hosting of, and attendance at, historical and other relevant lectures were a regular part of the rhythm of life at the Military Archives, including a visit from the US Military Academy at West Point's Cadet Pipe and Drum Band. In December 1995, Young was invited to the UK to present a paper at the Royal Military Academy, Sandhurst, indicative that he and the Archives had become players on the international stage and not just in Ireland. Relationships were formed and nurtured with sympathetic external agencies – the Military Heritage Trust of Ireland, the Military History Society of Ireland, University College Dublin, and the National Museum, were among many other historical societies, academic and cultural institutions with whom links were forged. As an interesting aside, particularly in light of the position of the Military Archives within the Intelligence Branch at that time, the Military History Society of Ireland, with its ethos of inclusive and pluralistic historical research, had for some years been regarded in diplomatic and intelligence circles as a positive force and ally in north / south relations.[18]

FILM WORK

One of Young's more unusual assignments came in the summer of 1994, when he was placed in charge of *No.1 Film Support Unit.* This unique unit was officially established on 1 July 1994 for the administration of military extras (both members of the permanent and reserve forces) for the movie *Braveheart,* following meetings and arrangements between Young and production executives both in Ireland and England from the previous May. This event is one that has become a part of Defence Forces, and particularly FCÁ (an Fórsa Cosanta Áitiúil – the designation of the Army reserve from 1946–2005), popular memory and lore. It is remembered fondly by those who were involved and Young himself described the troops involved with great affection: 'These lads were magic. Their discipline was excellent. They were able to organise much faster than civilians because they were so well trained and there weren't any serious injuries because they were disciplined.'[19]

As with everything he did, *No.1 Film Company* was treated with characteristic thoroughness and professionalism by Young. His post-production report to the Department of Defence detailed several challenges faced by the soldiers under his charge during the production, including in relation to pay, accommodation, welfare and catering. As it has been described, 'his concern for historical accuracy, and for the welfare of Army personnel involved, ensured that not all the battles that took place were on screen.'[20] This extended to his going on the record as being very critical of the film's lead actor, director and co-producer Mel Gibson, providing an intriguing, and amusing, insight into events.

> One lesson we quickly learned on 'Braveheart' was that unless it was written down and agreed beforehand, promises by the film company were not kept.

(1)   The extras would receive some memento of their time on set. A t-shirt was mentioned at an early stage. The 950 going away after the first week did receive a photo of Mel Gibson. None of the Core 500 received anything.

(2)   We were promised that there would be a day when families of those working on set could visit. This was never arranged.

(3)   We were promised that for one day we could bring cameras on set. We were never allowed to do so.

(4)   We were promised that Mel Gibson would have his photo taken with each platoon of the Core 500. This never materialised.

(5)   We were promised that Mel Gibson would visit the extras in the Dining Complex and Rugby Club. He never appeared.

(6)   We were promised an extra payment for the use of the Weapons School Complex. To date we have received nothing.

A lot of these broken promises and indeed problems on the set can be laid at the feet of Mel Gibson himself whose cavalier attitude to all did little to endear himself to anyone.[21]

Thankfully, this did not black-ball Young within the film industry. His skills remained in demand, and he was appointed as military liaison to the 1996 movie *Michael Collins*. This was a more straight-forward affair. Robert Fisk recalled how, while having dinner together one Friday, Young had invited him to drop by the set the following morning and be an extra in the filming of the first meeting of Dáil Éireann. Initially enthusiastic, Fisk recalled politely opting out when Young told him that they had to be on set at 7 a.m. that Saturday morning.

THE BUREAU OF MILITARY HISTORY

Of his many achievements, perhaps the one that has had the most comprehensive and enduring effects on historical research, was Young's role in securing the release of the records of the Bureau of Military History (BMH) into the custody of the Military Archives. The Bureau was established on 1 January 1947 by the Minister for Defence, Oscar Traynor. Its stated objective was 'to assemble and co-ordinate material to form the basis for the compilation of the history of the movement for Independence from the formation of the Irish Volunteers on 25 November 1913 to the 11 July 1921.'[22] Its definitive origins can be traced back to 1944, when Major Florence 'Florrie' O'Donoghue, the editor of *An Cosantóir*, suggested that the journal publish a series of articles on Irish military leaders. Growing out of this, at a meeting the following year between O'Donoghue, Colonel Dan Bryan, Robert Dudley Edwards and Richard Hayes, a plan authored by O'Donoghue was submitted to government. This was approved by the Taoiseach, Eamon de Valera and, once given the green light by the Department of Finance, the Bureau of Military History was established. However, the kernel of the BMH can be traced back to the early-1930s and various proposals and attempts to collect and preserve the records and memories of the struggle for Irish Independence, mentioned earlier in the book.

Michael McDunphy, Secretary to the President and a qualified lawyer, was appointed as the Director of the BMH in January 1947. The Bureau was administrated by the Defence Forces and staffed by a combination of military and civilian personnel. Florrie O'Donoghue, John McCoy and Seamus Robinson were full-time members and Colonel Dan Bryan was among the part-time members. These represented a cross section of both pro- and anti-Treaty veterans of the War of Independence. An advisory committee was also established, chaired by Richard F. Hayes and which included leading historians such as Robert Dudley Edwards, G.A. Hayes McCoy, Theodore W. Moody, Denis Gwynn, James Hogan and Richard J. Hayes.

Between 1947–1957, the Bureau's investigating officers recorded 1,773 witness statements from people who had taken part in military activities during the 1913–1921 period, travelling the length and breadth of the country, collecting from as broad a pool as possible. In this respect, the significance of the BMH, as described by Dr. Eve Morrison, was as 'a cultural initiative of the newly independent state to establish the bona fides of its claim to nationhood' and a 'symbol of republican reconciliation' arising from the antagonistic narratives that had arisen from the Civil War split.[23]

Initially, because of the sensitivity of some of the content within these statements, the government decided that they should be withheld from public inspection for twenty-five years (though those who made a statement were entitled to a copy and many of these had entered public circulation). They were kept in a strong room in the registry of the Department of the Taoiseach, with authority of access granted to the Minster for Defence. At the end of the initial twenty-five-year period, it was decided to review the decision on a five-yearly basis, which was then reduced to three-yearly. When a review came due in July of 1993, Young made representations to the government that the Military Archives would be the most suitable location for their care and custody.

Young rightly set the release of the BMH, as well as the Military Service Pensions files, firmly within his sights. He understood the significance of these records. He was not alone in this mission either, collaborating in his efforts with his friend and colleague Catriona Crowe of the National Archives. She recalled how:

> The two ghosts in the machine if you like, throughout all the years, were the Bureau of Military History and the Military Service Pensions files, and they became the *mission*, these *had* to be got out. With that we were facing the essential cautiousness of the Irish State around the Revolutionary period, and as we know we've had a fraught history relating to our past here, I mean…Irish history stopped for a lot of people in 1916, which was supposed to be the glorious revolution that suddenly morphed magically into independence. No mention of the War of Independence or the Civil War for quite a long time. So we were anxious that these very precious records be brought into the public domain.[24]

The BMH was not released in 1993. In anticipation of the next (1996) review, in August 1995 Young attended a meeting in Coláiste Caoimhín, Mobhi Road, Dublin, with representatives of the Department of Defence and National Archives to discuss a proposal to investigate the possible release of the Bureau of Military History papers. Yet again, in 1996, the BMH was not released.

1999: A BEGINNING AND AN END

1999 was a significant year for two reasons. It was the year that the government granted the release of the Bureau of Military History records to the custody Military Archives for public inspection. It was also the year the Peter Young died, suddenly and tragically, aged only forty-nine. Both events are linked in the minds of many of Young's friends and colleagues, but none more so than Catriona Crowe, who still vividly recalls the events of October 1999:

> The last time I saw Peter alive was the day we were summoned to the Department of the Taoiseach to be told that the Bureau records were to be released. We'd been campaigning for this, we'd enlisted historians to help us out. We'd always believed in building alliances with people outside the archives who could help us, so people like Diarmaid Ferriter, Eunan O'Halpin, Michael Hopkinson, Eve Morrison, all of those people who were historians of the period to which these records related were very anxious to help out with getting them released.
>
> So we were summoned in at 12 o'clock in the morning that day and we hoped for the best but we weren't sure what the consequences would be. Now remember, these records were held in a special strong room in Government Buildings, with two keys to the door – one held by the Minister for Defence, one held by the Taoiseach, so one without the other could never open them up. So, you know, we had made detailed submissions emphasising the passage of time since these records had been

created, downplaying any guarantees of confidentiality – which didn't really stand up when you looked at them anyway – Seán MacEoin in the Dáil saying they'd only be opened fifty years after all the people connected with these events were dead, that didn't seem to us to be a sufficiently strong guarantee to hold legal water. And there was huge demand for these records.

So anyway, we went in at 11 o'clock and we were told by the personnel of both departments that the records were going to be released forthwith, and that Peter should start preparing to have them brought to the Military Archives. We were thrilled! So we came out at 12 o'clock into the sunshine and we said we be better go and have a glass of whiskey because this was a historic day. We went down to the St Stephen's Green Hotel and we had a whiskey each, toasted the Bureau of Military History, left – I'd to go back to Bishop St and he to the Military Archives – and he turned around at the corner and blew me a kiss and that was the last time I saw him alive. He died a week later.

And that was it. It broke my heart. He was 49 years old, he had so much to offer. He was on the verge of this fantastic breakthrough which he would have so enjoyed and made the most of…[25]

PETER YOUNG'S LEGACY

Peter died suddenly from a heart issue on 27 October 1999, survived by his wife, Annette, and their four children: Eoghan, Ronan, Anne-Marie and Peter. While it was a life cut tragically short, it was also one marked by extraordinary achievement. In his final annual report, the Director of Intelligence had remarked that Young's:

> …achievements for the Defence Forces are more noteworthy considering how understaffed the archives section is and how cramped the surroundings are despite repeated cases for improvement. Commandant Young has the potential for, and is worthy of, future promotion.

The Assistant Chief of Staff, Brigadier General P.F. Nowlan, with whom Young had worked assiduously in developing a policy for the military section in the National Museum and the transfer of the Military Archives to the Collins Barracks site that failed to transpire, described Young's 'commitment to the policy of saving, and often rescuing, the record of Ireland's military heritage' as 'incomparable.'[26]

Incomparable is indeed the correct word. The Military Archives as it stands today, both physically and reputationally, is Commandant Peter Young's legacy. It is highly likely that the Military Archives would not exist today if it were not for Peter Young's intervention. This is only a part of his legacy though. Young influenced, and continues to influence, the ethos of the Military Archives through a combination of the power of personality and example. He is remembered warmly, it seems, by practically everyone with whom he crossed paths. Many of Ireland's most eminent historians recollect fond anecdotes when his name comes up in conversation. His Cadet School classmates recall his singular dedication to the Military Archives and his all-round competency as an officer. Friends and colleagues remember a great nature and someone not adverse to the occasional bit of rascality. Former members of the FCÁ still tell nostalgic stories of their time as part of *No.1 Film Support Unit* as extras on *Braveheart*, while others remember him from *Michael Collins*. All ranks who worked with Peter at the Archives are never shy of gently (and not so gently) reminding his successors that they have *very* big boots to try to fill. They are not wrong.

Young's obituary in the *Irish Times* noted that 'although he achieved an extraordinary amount in his 30 years of public service, he died with even greater possibilities opening in front of him.' This is true. It also said that 'his professional and military colleagues will be concerned to ensure that the future provides him with an adequate memorial.'

They most certainly were.

Chapter 7

1999–2012: THE COMMANDANT VICTOR LAING YEARS

Following the death of Commandant Peter Young, it fell to Commandant Victor Laing to take the reins and assume the appointment of Officer-in-Charge. Laing dedicated a significant portion of his military career to the Archives, foregoing opportunities for the benefit of the Military Archives, holding his appointment until his retirement in 2012. The immediate aftermath of Young's death was a precarious time for the Military Archives. Peter's strength of personality was as much a source of his success as his professional capacity. The Military Archives, as it had so many times in the past, could have fallen into inertia or obscurity following Young's death. The fact that it survived was down to Commandant Victor Laing.

The appointment of Staff Officer that Laing had previously occupied was now vacant. In June of 2000, it was filled by Captain Pat Brennan, whose prior appointment had been as the Administration Officer of the 8th Infantry Battalion (FCÁ). Brennan, like Laing and Young, was an intelligent and highly competent officer. He had previously been a senior NCO, holding the rank of Company Sergeant, before being commissioned from the ranks. Brennan had been selected for the Archives position from a pool of four applicants and began his necessary Higher

Diploma in Archives that September. At the same time, Laing had the foresight to recommended that the officer who had been ranked second in the competition, Captain Stephen Ryan, be sent on the Archives course in UCD the following year, in order to increase the extremely limited pool of professional archivists and providing some redundancy should one of the two officer appointments become vacant due to transfer, retirement or overseas service. Unfortunately, Laing was informed by the General Staff that the funding would not be forthcoming for Ryan to also undergo the course. Nonetheless, Ryan was an astute nomination by Laing. Holding the rank of Colonel and the appointment of Defence Forces Director of Operations at the time of writing, Ryan continues to maintain an interest in culture and heritage within the Defence Forces and a positive relationship with the Military Archives. He was, among other things, instrumental in establishing the collaboration between Stephens' Barracks, Kilkenny and the photographer Amelia Stein, which resulted in the acclaimed photography exhibition 'The Bloods', exhibited in the Butler Gallery in 2020.

2003: THE BUREAU OF MILITARY HISTORY RELEASED

While Laing was keeping an understaffed and under-resourced Military Archives afloat, the Bureau of Military History was still awaiting public release. In December 2002, the question of when the records would finally be released was raised in the Dáil by Sinn Féin's Deputy Aengus Ó Snodaigh.[1] As 2003 came around, the collection had still not been made available for public inspection. Conscious of potential repercussions, particularly in small communities with long memories, Laing was intent on ensuring that the material was thoroughly and carefully catalogued – and redacted as necessary in accordance with the statutory provisions of the National Archives Act[2] – before it would appear in the Reading Room. This brought Laing into constructive disagreement with his friend and colleague Catriona Crowe.

Crowe was of the opinion that the time spent in cataloguing by the Military Archives had been excessive, that 'there was a perfectly wonderful cataloguing system in existence already, created by [Bureau secretary] Paddy Brennan back in the 1950s – not a trained archivist but better than most trained archivists in terms of what he did because he knew the material.'[3] Both Crowe and Laing aired their concerns, and a compromise was reached, with the material released for public inspection in March 2003. Apprehension over the anticipated high public demand versus the limited capacity of the Military Archives Reading Room was mitigated by the duplicates of the Witness Statements being made available at the National Archives reading room in Bishop Street. In a show of good faith, David Craig, the Director of the National Archives at that time, provided £3,000 in funding for the launch of the collection – funding that had not been forthcoming from either the Defence Forces or Department of Defence.

HOLDING THE LINE

Despite the public prominence brought about by the release of the Bureau of Military History, the matter of suitable accommodation for the Military Archives remained unresolved. In 2003 an Interdepartmental Committee was established with terms of reference to examine and to advise on the best means of protecting and safeguarding the Military Archives by way of securing its removal from Cathal Brugha Barracks to a new premises to be developed at Collins Barracks, Dublin, by this time evacuated of military personnel and a functioning National Museum site. Reporting to the Minister for Defence, the Committee's membership was drawn from the Department of Defence (civilian and military), the Department of Arts, Sport and Tourism, the Office of Public Works, the National Archives, the National Museum, and the Military Heritage Trust.

Later that same year and into 2004, Laing found himself again as the only officer at the Archives, as Brennan was deployed on an overseas mission to Kosovo with the 27th Infantry Group, KFOR. In May 2004, Laing attended an Interdepartmental Committee Meeting at Defence Forces Headquarters to discuss the development of the National Museum at Collins Barracks and the ongoing issue of the co-location of the Archives. This meeting was chaired by Conor Kerlin of the Department of Defence, with representatives present from all the departments that constituted the committee and BDP Architects.

At this meeting, Chris Flynn, of the Department of Arts, Culture, Tourism and Sport, informed those present that the Secretary General of his Department (Phil Furlong) had met just prior to the meeting with his counterpart in the Department of Defence (David O'Callaghan) and discussed the matter of the Military Archives being merged with the National Archives. Furthermore, he informed the meeting that Pat Wallace, the Director of the National Museum, now no longer wanted the Military Archives located at the Collins Barracks site – a complete U-turn from his previous position. To make matters worse, all of this had been done without consulting or informing Laing.

Laing stood his ground and challenged the fact that decisions were apparently being made about the future of the Military Archives in advance and outside of the Interdepartmental Committee. In this position, Laing was supported by the Director of the National Archives, who objected to the suggestion of such a merger as unfeasible and one which would require the unnecessary revocation of the Military Archives statutory designation as a 'place of deposit.' Had this come to fruition the work of the Military Archives over the past decades would have been undone. Had Laing not been there to hold the line as the Military Archives' director, that could well have come to pass.

It was now clear that the move to the Collins Barracks site was becoming increasingly unlikely. Laing, however, had a plan for this contingency and this episode proved the catalyst for his proposing that the Military Archives be redeveloped on a site within Cathal Brugha Barracks itself. To do so, he considered, would provide far fewer restrictions than an external site. Laing's vision was for an archival facility suitable for use

Former barracks hospital block, after suffering fire damage in February 1968, while in use by the Army School of Music. The block now houses the Reading Room and offices of the Military Archives. *Credit: Image provided by Sergeant PJ Lydon, Defence Forces School of Music.*

Commandant Peter Young and Captain Victor Laing (2nd and 3rd from left) at the Military Archives inspecting the restored banner carried by the National Army at the handover of Portobello (later Cathal Brugha) Barracks. The banner was in the custody of Kilmainham Jail and was identified as the banner carried at the handover by Sgt Joe White of the Military Archives. *Credit: The Military Archives.*

Renovation of the old barrack hospital block as the reading room and offices of new Military Archives building. 2015. *Credit: The Military Archives.*

Installation of shelving units in the repository block of the new Military Archives building. 2015. *Credit: The Military Archives.*

Construction of the new Military Archives building. Poured concrete sign being lowered into place. 2015. *Credit: The Military Archives.*

New Military Archives building immediately following construction, March 2016. *Credit: The Military Archives.*

Vice Admiral Mark Mellet (Chief of Staff), President Michael D. Higgins, Brigadier General Michael Beary, at the official opening of the new Military Archives building, 26 April 2016. *Credit: Gary Murphy (Defence Forces Corps of Engineers), The Military Archives.*

Media interest and guests at the official opening of the new Military Archives building, 26 April 2016. *Credit: Gary Murphy (Defence Forces Corps of Engineers), The Military Archives.*

Above: President
Michael D. Higgins,
speaking at the official
opening of the new
Military Archives build-
ing, 26 April 2016.

Right: Catriona Crowe,
National Archives of
Ireland, speaking at the
official opening of the
new Military Archives
building, 26 April
2016. *Both images
credit: Gary Murphy
(Defence Forces Corps
of Engineers), The
Military Archives.*

Above: Commandant Padraic Kennedy, while Director of the Military Archives, speaking at the official opening of the new Military Archives building, 26 April 2016.

Below: President Michael D. Higgins, officially opening the new Military Archives building, 26 April 2016. *Both image credit: Gary Murphy (Defence Forces Corps of Engineers), The Military Archives.*

Above: Commandant Padraic Kennedy, Dr Ristéard Mulcahy (son of General Richard Mulcahy), Commandant Victor Laing (retired) and Commandant Stephen Mac Eoin, at the opening of the new Military Archives building.

Below: Conservatory Audrey McGinley working on a War of Independence era Proclamation of Martial Law from the Brother Allen Collection, at the Military Archives conservation laboratory. *Credit: The Military Archives.*

Left: Robert Fisk, pictured with the author and archivists.
Credit: The Military Archives

Below: Visit to the Military Archives of Dublin football manager and former Army officer, Jim Gavin, with the Sam Maguire cup. L-R: Sergeant Gerry McCann (retired), Jim Gavin, Lisa Dolan, Quartermaster Sergeant Tom Mitchell, Sergeant David 'Ned' Kelly, Hugh Beckett, Noelle Grothier.
Credit: Commandant Stephen Mac Eoin.

Right: Key individuals responsible for the Military Service Pensions Collection, photographed at the event marking the project's 10th anniversary in 2018. L-R Commandant Pat Brennan, Brigitta O'Doherty (Department of Defence), Cécile Gordon (Project Manager), Maurice Quinn (Secretary General). *Credit: Cécile Gordon.*

Below: Commandant Victor Laing (3rd from left) one of 6 recipients of honorary doctorates from UCD in 2016, for advancing Ireland's understanding of the revolutionary period. To his left is Catriona Crowe. *Credit: Colm Mahady, courtesy of University College Dublin.*

Above and below: Military Archives Oral History Project team in South Lebanon, 2018. The team spent a week collecting testimony as part of the 40th anniversary of the first Irish Defence Forces deployment to Lebanon as part of the United Nations Interim Force in Lebanon (UNIFIL). Photo above features L-R: Cpl Michael Whelan, Noelle Grothier, Lisa Dolan, Comdt Daniel Ayiotis, Sgt David 'Ned' Kelly. Photo below features Lisa Dolan and Noelle Grothier in helmet and body armour, preparing to travel with military convoy. *Credit: The Military Archives.*

by the public and military, situated on the Defence Forces own real estate, which would be representative of the pride that the military had in looking after its own material and how the organisation projected itself externally. For Laing, such a manifestation of the Military Archives would be an incredibly positive and strong statement for the Defence Forces.[4]

SETTLING ON A SUITABLE LOCATION

The matter of relocating and staffing the Military Archives was raised regularly in Dáil Debates between 2005–2006. Laing's anticipation that a new site would have to be considered was vindicated in 2006, when the Minister for Defence, Seán Barrett, conceded that in relation to the Collins Barracks site:

> …difficulties have arisen. Initially the architectural consultants produced three reports outlining the pros and cons — mostly cons — of certain locations within Collins Barracks. Subsequently, in January 2005, the consultants produced two further reports. Difficulties have arisen in respect of all the proposed locations and I have therefore revitalised and reactivated the interdepartmental committee and asked it to extend its search beyond Collins Barracks. It is more or less understood and I can confirm that the search will not extend beyond Dublin. I have sent word to the interdepartmental committee, and intend to tell its members personally that I want a range of options by the end of the summer, at which time we will have to decide on one option or a combination thereof.[5]

2005–2009: CHANGES

In December 2005, Pat Brennan, by then holding the rank of Commandant, retired from the Defence Forces. Arguably his retirement only five years after his selection for the appointment and four years after his attaining the formal qualification necessary to fill it, vindicated Laing's previous advocacy on behalf of Captain Stephen Ryan to also undergo professional archival training. While Brennan's erstwhile appointment was not immediately filled, in 2006 Commandant Billy Campbell was given a one-year posting on attachment as Laing's deputy.

Campbell was interested in history since childhood, something he brought with him to the Defence Forces as a regular contributor to the likes of *An Cosantóir* and the *Defence Forces Review*. In 2000, he decided to develop his interest and completed a part-time BA in History and Geography at UCD over six years. Campbell was planning on retiring as a Commandant in 2007 and, having decided that the next logical step was to undertake an MA in Archives and Records Management, he requested a posting to the Military Archives for his final year in service to get the necessary pre-course experience.

Campbell, who had been in Laing's senior Cadet Class, was a welcome addition. While he thoroughly loved every minute that he was there, he still recalled the chronic understaffing and under-resourcing that the Military Archives was enduring:

> The staff was minimal – Victor and Private Alan Manning, and that was basically it. I arrived and Victor said: 'you will do the correspondence, you'll answer the written queries from the public, and I will take care of the actual visitors to the place.' So, I opened the file and I discovered that it was a year behind, I was dealing with 2005's queries. But again, I managed to bring it up to date in the year I was there. Now, unfortunately, by the time I left, there was no one to take over from me, so it was back to the old way again.[6]

Despite still being under-resourced, 2006 proved to be an auspicious year for the Military Archives. An event took place that, possibly through *the law of unintended consequences*, would eventually contribute to the establishment of the Archives of the type Young and Laing had always intended.

It was during this year, the ninetieth anniversary of the 1916 Easter Rising, that Taoiseach Bertie Ahern announced the decision to afford public access to the *Military Service (1916–1923) Pensions Collection (MSPC)*.

This collection, described as 'the single most important archival collection relating to Ireland's revolutionary period,'[7] originated in a government decision in June 1923 to recognise and compensate wounded members, and the widows, children and dependents of deceased members, of the Irish Volunteers, Irish Citizen Army, Irish Republican Army and National Army. Over the years, the remit of the pensions expanded to include Cumann na mBan, Fianna Éireann, the Hibernian Rifles and those members of the Connaught Rangers who had mutinied in India in 1920.

In 2007, an MSPC Steering Committee was established, chaired by the Department of the Taoiseach with representatives from the Department of Defence, the Defence Forces, the National Archives and the Military Archives. By the following year, four civilian archivists were recruited for this project. Commandant Pat Brennan, now a civilian, returned to the Military Archives as the project manager. He was joined by Cécile Chemin (who would eventually succeed him as Project Manager), Michael Keane and Pat Long (later replaced by Robert McEvoy). While a part of the Military Archives and acting under the statutory authority of the institution as a place of deposit under the terms of the National Archives Act, the MSPC Project Team worked solely on the project as a discrete entity, reporting to a member of Executive Branch, Department of Defence as Line Manager, while the Officer-in-Charge of the Military Archives sat on the project Steering Committee. As part of this recruitment of civilian staff, the first civilian archivists to join the Military Archives itself were recruited at the same time. These were Hugh Beckett, Lisa Dolan and Noelle Grothier.

Questions regarding staffing, accommodation, public access and the release of files continued to be raised regularly in Dáil Debates. However, from 2008 and the beginning of the MSPC project, there was an interesting change in the language of the responses from the Minister in relation to the need for suitable accommodation:

The requirement for a more suitable home for the Military Archives has been recognised for some time and has been the subject of significant research. *The long-term accommodation for the Military Archives will be reviewed in the context of the Military Pensions Archive project.*[8] [Italics own]

CAPTAIN STEPHEN MAC EOIN

2007 also saw the arrival at the Military Archives of Captain Stephen Mac Eoin. Mac Eoin had returned from an overseas deployment to Kosovo in March of that year and was posted to the Military Archives, having successfully applied for the position, in order to gain necessary practical experience before undertaking the MA in Archives and Records Management in UCD from September of that year. Like Young and Laing before him, he threw himself into the work, and gained a positive reputation for his enthusiasm and competence within the Defence Forces as well as the archival and wider heritage professions. Mac Eoin worked prolifically in the field. He was appointed to the Expert Advisory Group of Commemorations, established by the Taoiseach in 2011 to advise the government on historical matters relevant to the Decade of Centenaries, and between 2015 and 2016 he was seconded as the Defence Forces liaison officer to the *Ireland 2016* team, working under the auspices of the Department of Arts, Heritage and the Gaeltacht. Following this secondment, he returned in 2017, holding the rank of Commandant, to fill the appointment of Officer-in-Charge of the Military Archives for just under a year.

GAINING MOMENTUM

As the first decade of the twenty-first century ended and the *Decade of Centenaries* loomed large on the national horizon, the Military Archives was slowly beginning to come into the ascendency. It had a director and deputy director in Laing and Mac Eoin, as well as qualified civilian archivists in Beckett, Dolan and Grothier. In parallel, the MSPC project had been stood-up, staffed, and was progressing through the substantial task of preparing for its first release, which would happen in 2014.

The political momentum was growing too. The matters of suitable accommodation and releases of material were regularly raised in the Oireachtas. There were visits, for example, from Deputy Jimmy Deenihan of Fine Gael and Senator Ceceila Keaveney of Fianna Fáil, the latter reporting afterwards in the Seanad that:

> I recently visited the Military Archives in Cathal Brugha Barracks, Dublin, and was thrilled to come across a group photograph which includes my grandfather. I also discovered his original autograph in the Ballykinlar book. It was a thrill to see the autograph of my grandfather, who died before I was born. I encourage the Minister to find mechanisms to provide more such research locations for students and others. The authorities at the military archives told me that they have boxes of material that they cannot record. The archival material is lying in warehouses because they do not have the personnel to deal with it. While there may be data protection issues involved, there are many students who would like to have an opportunity to access that material. I thank the House for allowing me some latitude to raise that issue.[9]

In early 2010, while Laing was posted to Bosnia with the 11th Irish Component, EUFOR, Mac Eoin acted in his place as archive director. During this time the matter of accommodation and public access remained politically live, with Deputies Richard Bruton (Fine Gael) and Kathleen Lynch (Labour Party) requesting progress updates from the Minster for Defence in February and April's Dáil Debates. The Minister for Defence provided the usual stock reply that 'the long-term accommodation for the Military Archive will be reviewed in the context of the military pension archive project.'

Behind the scenes the machinery was starting to move. In December 2010, the Minister for Defence, Deputy Tony Kileen (Fianna Fáil), informed the House that the Secretary General of the Department of Defence had granted an Exceptional Performance Award for the sum of €1,500 to an Assistant Principal in his Department in recognition of 'exceptional performance while working on the Judicial Reviews and the Military Archives Pensions Project.'[10] While this was no doubt deserved, the Military Archives itself was still struggling with funding – as one of the archivists recalled in confidence 'there were times in those days when we didn't even have the budget to buy paperclips.'

That same month, the Chief of Staff, Lieutenant General Seán McCann, visited the Military Archives and received a brief from Laing. A part of this visit, Laing brought McCann to the old barracks' Hospital Block, which had been identified at that stage as the potential future location for the Military Archives.

By 2011, momentum was still building, both internally and externally, and the future of the Military Archives was, tentatively, looking bright. There were on average twenty-one members of the public visiting the Archives each week in 2011. Laing and his team also received on average sixty phone calls and thirty-five letters and emails per week. However, the delivery of the necessary support and development of the Military Archives was not a *fait accompli* at the political level. In Dáil questions the Taoiseach, Enda Kenny, said in reference to the *Military Service Pensions Collection*, that 'we plan to have those 300,000 files available to the public long before 2016'[11] indicating either poor advice or a stunning naivety regarding the reality of the work of archival cataloguing and digitisation. The necessary research into the pensions legislation, unravelling and understanding complexities of the record management system uses, and identifying and locating the requisite files alone took the project team several years. There was even direct, and seemingly petty, antagonism towards the Military Archives from Labour's Deputy Kevin Humphreys, who asked the Minister for Defence to make a statement to the Dáil relating to the cost of publishing and distributing the Military Archives 2012 Calendar and whether he viewed this spend of €2,677 as 'an appropriate use of scarce resources.'[12] The calendar, as the Minister explained, formed an integral part of the Military Archives outreach programme, and the 2012 calendar was distributed as a promotional tool at the launch of a significant initiative that came to fruition that year – going online.

In December 2011, the Military Archives website went live for the first time. Success bred success and by the middle of the year the Minster for Defence, Alan Shatter (Fine Gael), announced that:

> Following the launch of the website in December 2011 the average number of emails more than doubled while there was a 30–40% increase in phone calls. The average number of visitors per week had increased to twenty-seven. In addition to the use by the public there are on average 35 written queries per week from military personnel. It is expected that the coming twelve months will see a further increase in the workload of the Archive staff as 2013 marks the 100th anniversary of the Irish Volunteers. The current workload also includes the transfer and cataloguing of collections from various military sources along with answering queries from the public and military users.[13]

THE BOARD TO EXAMINE MILITARY ARCHIVES

2011 was also the year that an important report concerning the future of the Military Archives was published. *The Board Assembled to Examine Military Archives*[14] was primarily a military board, presided over by Colonel Brian Reade and featuring Laing and Mac Eoin, but which also had Department of Defence representation in Brigitta O'Doherty, and Catriona Crowe of the National Archives as a consultant. The Board was initiated by O'Doherty as a DoD representative on the Military Service Pensions Collection Project Steering Committee, a staunch supporter of the MSPC and the requirement for a new building. The Board was established with a view to ascertaining the finer details of what the development of the Military Archives, which was gaining serious momentum but had until then only really been discussed generally, would entail.

The Board's terms of reference included: conducting a review and make recommendations on the Archives' current and future storage facilities; making recommendations on the feasibility of establishing such a facility at a civilian location while retaining the traditional military linkage; making recommendations on the military and civilian staff ratios with consideration to the traditional military control of such a facility; and any other matters deemed relevant by the Board.

The Board's report repeated and reinforced the refrain of previous Ministers for Defence over the recent years, that 'the key to providing suitable accommodation and infrastructure for the Military Archives lay in the Military Service Pensions Collection.'[15] The Board also reported that the physical arrangement for accessing the records in the custody of the Military Archives was inadequate. With the impending release of the *Military Service Pensions Collection* in particular, as a cornerstone of the government's 2016 centenary events, it was clear that the awareness of, and demand for, military records in general was going to increase dramatically.

At the time of the Board's report, the issue of the requirement for an adequate building to facilitate public access and appropriate storage was being pursued centrally. As they noted, the development of such a facility could not be funded by the Department of Defence and would have to be provided from central Government. To address this, the Steering Committee provided a series of options to the Office of Public Works, including the refurbishment of the Hospital Block in Cathal Brugha Barracks as office and reading-room space and the construction of a purpose-built archival repository. Furthermore, the Steering Committee's recommendation that the government make five-million euro available for this purpose as part of the 2016 Centenary Commemoration Programme, was strongly supported by the Department of the Taoiseach.

While the report covered a wide range of topics, including the archiving of digital records and medical records, which have been implemented to very limited degrees, the proposal for the investment and infrastructure were precisely what came to be. The report remains a useful reference and planning document for Officers-in-Charge of the Military Archives. The Board was also prescient in its recommendation of the value of relocating the Military Archives from under the remit of Intelligence Branch to Public Relations Branch. It noted the opportunity for the Defence Forces and Department of Defence to capitalise on its PR potential, which would become more evident as the centenary of the 1916 Rising approached. One other particularly interesting recommendation, inserted at her own request, was the unilateral recommendation of the Departmental representative 'that consideration should be given in the context of the current re-organisation of the DF to the possible civilianisation of the staff of the Military Archives.'[16]

THE BUREAU OF MILITARY HISTORY ONLINE

2012 saw the release of the *Bureau of Military History* witness statements online, though this was on its own dedicated website, a collaboration between the Military Archives and the National Archives. This was the beginning of a revolutionary development in terms of the accessibility and availability of the Military Archives' records, one which would grow even more dramatically with the first release of material from the *Military Service Pensions Collection* two years later. It was a democratisation of history in a sense, facilitating unprecedented access, insight and nuance of understanding of Irish revolutionary history.

With the late Peter Young's aspiration having come to fruition, of the Bureau of Military History records being released from under lock-and-key in Government Buildings and publicly accessibly in the custody of the Military Archives, the project began shortly after to have the collection digitised and made available online. Catriona Crowe recalls:

> Then the work began to try to get them online. I managed to get the money out of our Department – Defence wasn't going to pony out for it. The Department of Arts, Heritage and whatever it was at the time – Niall

Ó Donnchú, a really great civil servant who saw the value of it, gave us the money to digitise and we did that and got it online, and that again gave it a huge lease of life among people who might not be able or willing to come to the National Archives or the Military Archives. And that meant we could put away the originals, which is the idea and another reason why digitisation is useful – it stops wear and tear on the originals when you put them online. And put online to the best standard, with a good catalogue, linked to the original document. That is best practice. And it had variations on things too, plenty of essays to contextualise the material and that... I must say it was just joy all the way with the Bureau. It was *wonderful* to get them finally out into the open and see the reaction that people had.

COMMANDANT VICTOR LAING RETIRES

2012 was a significant year for another reason – while the Military Archives had gained so much under his direction, this was the year that Commandant Victor Laing retired from the Defence Forces. Laing's dedication had ensured not only that the Military Archives survived but that it prospered. In 2016, his efforts were formally recognised when he was one of six people conferred with an Honorary PhD from UCD as part of the college's Decade of Centenaries programme for work that has improved public understanding of the formation and development of the Irish State. In Laing's case, this was in relation to the release of the Bureau of Military History. Dr Conor Mulvagh's citation is as generally applicable to Laing's legacy at the Military Archives as it is specifically to his work with the digitisation of the Bureau of Military History.

As Officer Commanding Irish Military Archives, Victor presided over one of the most remarkable and extensive archival digitisation projects in the history of the State...I would argue, and I believe it is not an overstate-ment to say, that this achievement remains one of the most incredible feats of vision, perseverance, and commitment in Irish archival history.

Chapter 8

2012–2016: THE MODERN
MILITARY ARCHIVES

The Military Archives entered the most recent decade of its existence (as it stands at the time of writing) under the leadership of
Commandant Padraic Kennedy, who took over from Laing in
August of 2012 following his academic and professional qualification as
an archivist. The Military Archives came to the awareness of Kennedy
somewhat serendipitously. He recalled in interview[1] how, having finished
a tour of duty as a platoon commander on Ireland's final deployment to
East Timor,[2] that it had been clear to him that there were a lot of important files and reports generated by the Irish contingent that needed to be
returned to the Military Archives. Separately, he had formed an awareness
of the Military Archives and its work through his father, himself a former
Army officer, who had encouraged him to donate his Cadet uniform to
the Archives' uniform collection.[3] His father was the Officer-in-Charge of
the Defence Forces' Enlisted Personnel Section at the time that a large-
scale project to microfilm personnel records had been initiated – the
digitised versions of which are still in regular use by the Military Archives.

The appointment was not Kennedy's first practical experience with
the Military Archives either. He had dealt regularly with Laing and his
team during his previous appointment in Public Relations Branch, when
he was the Officer-in-Charge of the Information Office and manager
of *An Cosantóir* magazine. This necessitated regular contact in relation

to both public queries to the Information Office and historical queries relating to articles in the magazine.

This prior experience stood to Kennedy. Only a week after taking up his appointment, the *Bureau of Military History* was launched online. The associated public interest and requests for interviews forced Kennedy to rapidly get established and familiarise himself with the finer points of the collection and his broader role as the archive director.

In 2012, the Defence Forces underwent another reorganisation, and while this would have positive impacts for the Military Archives, it had not yet come into effect, so Kennedy was still working with reduced military staff. Mac Eoin departed for overseas service and his replacement, Captain Claire Mortimer, was undertaking her MA in Archives and Records Management in UCD.

Kennedy inherited an institution that Laing had left on an upward trajectory, but 2012 was also a year of significant change. Under the reorganisation of the Defence Forces, the Military Archives was removed from the Intelligence Branch and placed within the Public Relations Branch, situating it directly under the Chief of Staff, as opposed to the Deputy Chief of Staff (Operations) where Intelligence had sat. This had been recommended previously[4] and was a better fit within the organisation. The Military Archives was now a progressive institution providing an increasingly availed-of face-to-face public service with a statutory mandate. It was also part of a wider archival profession which had an ethos based on being outward-looking agents of state accountability and citizen advocacy through the provision of access to the documentary evidence of decisions made by the state on citizens' behalf.

Under this reorganisation the staffing of the Military Archives was also revised. Captain Claire Mortimer was identified as a replacement for Captain Stephen Mac Eoin in 2012, although only took over properly following her return from UCD in August of 2013. In the meantime, Kennedy resourcefully established an interim arrangement by requesting a temporary administration and project officer. This role was filled by Lieutenant Deirdre Carbery in February 2013.

New NCO appointments were created too. The senior most of these was Quartermaster, filled by Tom Mitchell; Admin Sergeant, filled by David 'Ned' Kelly; and Stores Corporal, filled by Andrew Lawlor. The only negative aspect was that the appointment of Private Storeman / Driver, which had been filled by Adrian Short since 2008, was removed from the establishment. Short was allowed to remain 'on attachment' from the 7th Infantry Battalion. While the staffing levels were a significant improvement on the past, they were still below those recommended by the 2011 *Report of the Defence Forces Board Assembled to Examine Military Archives.* This Board had recommended a military establishment of three officers (a Commandant Officer-in-Charge and two Captains – one Archivist and one Admin officer), a CQMS, Sergeant, and two Privates.

2013: ENTERING THE DECADE OF CENTENARIES

As the state entered the Decade of Centenaries, the tempo at the Military Archives naturally increased. November 2013 marked the centenary of the foundation of the Irish Volunteers, (the predecessor organisation to which the modern Irish Defence Forces traces its direct lineage) and the Military Archives was heavily involved in the event, including being tasked with designing and producing an exhibition of historical panels. This, as one may suspect, is somewhat outside the remit of an archivist. Kennedy had to rapidly go from being an archivist to a heritage professional and historian – highlighting the misconception still held my many inside and outside of the Defence Forces that OIC Military Archives is an historian, and the broad expectations that are implicit in holding the appointment. On the other hand, the multi-talented and versatile Peter Young had arguably established this as the template for those who would follow in the office he had fought to re-establish. That said, Kennedy proved himself a versatile leader too, and was responsible for introducing a range of digitisation initiatives and the ground-breaking *Military Archives Oral History Project* during his tenure.

Throughout 2013, the Military Archives remained a live issue in the Dáil. In May of that year, the Taoiseach, Enda Kenny (Fine Gael), was questioned about the development of Moore Street – the site of the final stand and surrender of the leaders of the 1916 Easter Rising – by Deputy Gerry Adams of Sinn Féin. While possibly an oblique reference, it is worthwhile to examine the high-level context within which the Military Archives was now being discussed, less than a decade after the Department of Defence were proposing having it merged with the National Archives and, in effect, dissolving it.

Mr Adams' proposition to the Taoiseach was as follows:

> Moore Street is a monument of which one is not proud. I visited it and it is not the kind of site to which one would like to refer people as the last headquarters of those who left the GPO by the side door in 1916. It is a complex matter involving developers, Dublin City Council, the Minister and NAMA etc. I have asked the Minister to prepare a memo for Government because we must make a decision. The Minister can intervene in law, but any intervention should take into account what we want for the general area by the time we get to 2016. As I said to other Deputies, I would like to think we could do something about the Military Archives, the courthouse in Kilmainham, the GPO itself and the national monument in Moore Street. The Minister will bring his memo to Government shortly. It is a matter which can be discussed in the House. The Minister has a particular interest in the matter as chair of the centenary commemoration events. It is a case of ensuring any intervention is the right one in the context of what the nation wants for the national monument at Moore Street.

Mr Adams' related remarks in a follow up debate, that 'the sites the Taoiseach mentioned, such as...the military archives, are not under any threat'[5] was only partially accurate. The momentum and support was there at that time, but as the previous century had repeatedly illustrated, the fortunes of the Military Archives rose and fell based on the patronage and indulgence of those in military and political authority.

2014: CERTAINTY AT LAST

In January 2014, the first tranche of material from the *Military Service Pensions Collection* was released online to a rapturous reception from historians and public alike. By December of that year, the weight of support for the Military Archives – from within the Defence Forces, Department of Defence, politics, and academia, finally reached critical mass. Deputy Heather Humphries of Fine Gael, the Minister for Arts, Heritage and the Gaeltacht, announced in the Seanad that:

> Earlier this year, additional funding of €22 million for 2015 was secured for a number of flagship commemoration projects. These include the GPO interpretative centre, Kilmainham Courthouse and Gaol, the Military Archives, Teach an Phiarsaigh in Ros Muc, the Tenement Museum, Richmond Barracks, and redevelopment works at the National Concert Hall. Each of these projects will deepen our understanding of the history of that period and will provide a permanent tribute to those involved in the Rising. They are also a key component of Ireland 2016, a national initiative led by my Department to mark the 100th anniversary of 1916 in an inclusive, appropriate and respectful way.[6]

The vision of Commandants Peter Young and Victor Laing, for a Military Archives that reflected the significance of the records it held to the foundation and story of the Irish state, was going to become a reality.

The Military Archives was finally being formally recognised as the immensely important site of national memory that it was. The project would be one of nine 'Permanent Reminders' – Government of Ireland capital projects as part of the Decade of Centenaries commemorative programme. Kennedy was to be the Officer-in-Charge who would be responsible for the transition of its staff and collections. They were still headquartered in the not fit-for-purpose St Patrick's Hall with a large amount of the Archives' holdings stored in insulated and humidity-controlled containers throughout Cathal Brugha Barracks but also in other locations including a categorically unsuitable site in the Curragh Camp. Many tens of thousands more records, particularly, but not exclusively, personnel files dating back as far as 1922, remained stockpiled in the various administrative headquarters around the country awaiting transfer. Now the Military Archives would be headquartered in the fully renovated barracks hospital block with a purpose built, climate-controlled repository with over twenty-one linear kilometres of shelving. The project would be carried out by Irish architectural firm McCullough Mulvin, with Corán O'Connor appointed as the lead architect.

THE MOVE

2015 proved a hectic time for Kennedy and his team – not only were they busy with various taskings related the various ongoing centenaries, not least the approaching centenary of the Easter Rising itself, but once the building was complete, they only had a few months to start transferring records and setting up their workspace with all necessities required. While the transfer and accession of material would, in reality, take several more years, they were ready to open in time for the official opening.

Tuesday 26 April 2016 was the date of the official opening ceremony. This was presided over, fittingly, by President Michael D Higgins – not only an accomplished academic and intellectual, but the Supreme Commander of the Irish Defence Forces. Kennedy, as Officer-in-Charge, was one of the people who would address those in attendance. This audience included many of the people who had supported the project and brought it to that very day. Kennedy recalled that, before he gave his address, being taken aside by the then Secretary General of the Department of Defence, Maurice Quinn, and in no uncertain terms, informed that he was not to neglect to include the Department of Defence in his acknowledgements of those responsible for bringing this project to fruition. Quinn was, without a doubt, a consummate supporter of the project, and without his Department's support, it would most likely not have happened. However, given the preceding history of his Department's disposition towards the Military Archives, trying to withdraw Departmental records from its custody in 1990 and trying to have its statutory mandate revoked and merged with the National Archives in 2004, perhaps a more humble attitude may have been apt?

In his address, President Higgins described how, through the establishment of the new Military Archives 'we have secured the story of our past but also that we have left it open to further contributions...It will just grow and grow and I think that future generations will be grateful for it. It's a great, great credit to those who made it possible.[7] It was, he said, 'a fitting recognition of the fundamental importance of the Military Archives towards our understanding of the founding events of the state.'[8]

Epilogue

THE PRESENT

In 2016, Kennedy finished his tenure at the Military Archives and departed for a new appointment. He was replaced by Stephen Mac Eoin, now a Commandant, as the Officer-in-Charge. Captain Claire Mortimer left this same year, replaced as Staff Officer by Captain Daniel Ayiotis, who had been selected for the post the previous year and returned from undertaking the prerequisite MA in Archives and Records Management in UCD that July. Around the same time, Corporal Andrew Lawlor was replaced by Corporal Kevin Byrne. There were further changes in 2017, when Mac Eoin departed to take up an appointment in the Cadet School. This left Ayiotis as the acting Officer-in-Charge until his promotion to Commandant in April 2019, when he was appointed substantively. 2019 also saw the selection of Captain Sarah Colclough for appointment to the Staff Officer vacancy. Until then an Air Traffic Controller in the Air Corps, Colclough, in a fitting example of circularity, is the great grand nice of Michael McDunphy, the Director of the Bureau of Military History.

2018 saw the retirement of Adrian Short, and the following year Sergeant David Kelly followed suit, while Kevin Byrne transferred to the Corps of Engineers. Short could not be replaced as there had not been a Private's appointment on the establishment of the Archives since the reorganisation in 2012. Kelly and Byrne, however, were replaced by Sergeant Matthew Weafer and Corporal Joseph McDermott in 2019. Both of these new NCOs were very welcome additions to the team, bringing with them firmly established reputations for initiative, reliability, common sense and hard work. Weafer's previous appointment had been in the Defence Forces Freedom of Information office, a section in regular contact with the Archives, so his appointment was a natural cross-pollination of skills within the organisation. McDermott's preceding appointment had been in a logistical accountancy role, which along with a wide range of driving qualifications, further expanded the Archives' pool of skills.

Cécile Chemin, who had been acting Project Manager for the Military Service Pensions Collection project since Pat Brennan had retired in 2017, was officially appointed as Project Manager and Senior Archivist in 2019. In 2020, three more civilian archivists were hired by the Department of Defence – Sam McGrath and Leanne Ledwidge being posted to the MSPC project team and Linda Hickey being posted to the main Military Archives. Hickey departed to take up a position as the Senior Archivist at Dublin City Library and Archives in 2022 and Aislinn Mohan became the most recent addition to the team Separately, the Department of Defence took on their own archivist in 2019, based at their headquarters in Newbridge. Evelyn McAuley's task, ongoing at the time of writing, is to survey and catalogue the current backlog of Departmental records (the Archives series of departmental records at time of writing end around 1970) and arrange their deposit at the Military Archives. All-in-all, between the Defence Forces and Department of Defence, there are ten civilian archivists currently employed. This is to the credit of both organisations and an example to the wider public and civil service.

The final members of the team are the Military Archives' corps of volunteers. While many have passed through the doors over the years, the Military Archives currently benefits from the experience and generosity of Lieutenant Colonel Richard Cummins (retired), Colonel Tom Hodson (retired), Tony Kinsella, Sergeant Gerry McCann (retired), Flight Sergeant James Perkins (retired) and, still going strong after more than three decades, Denis McCarthy.

BROADENING HORIZONS

The Decade of Centenaries brought the Military Archives into an ascendant position within the Irish cultural, historical and heritage landscape. This is evident, for example, from the decision by the Christian Brothers of O'Connell School, Richmond Road, to donate the *Brother Allen Collection* to the Military Archives as a gift to the State in 2016. This astonishing collection of documents and artefacts – assembled over many years by the Cork-born Brother William Allen – comprises approximately 13,000 items – from early Irish history right through to the revolutionary period and into the mid-twentieth century. An anecdotal example of the richness and national importance of the collection is the fact that over eighty items from the Brother Allen Collection were on loan to the National Museum of Ireland as part of their *Proclaiming a Republic* exhibition.

There is now greater awareness and understanding of the Military Archives and its roles both within the Defence Forces and Department of Defence, and among the wider public. This increase in support and resourcing has allowed the Military Archives to broaden its horizons and fully engage within the archival and wider heritage professions.

A primary example of this is the *Oral History Project*. This was established in 2015 by Commandant Padraic Kennedy during his tenure. Dr Tomás Mac Conmara, an award-winning oral historian and author, was contracted to design the methodology and conduct the training, with archivist Noelle Grothier as the project manager. The aim of the project, which is ongoing, is to digitally record the memory, oral history and tradition associated with the Defence Forces since its inception.

While there was a broad call for volunteer interviewers throughout the Defence Forces, the vast majority of the work has been conducted by Corporal Michael Whelan of the Air Corps. Whelan, a historian, poet, author and curator of the Air Corps Museum, has, at the time of writing, collected in excess of three-hundred interviews. Quite simply, if it were not for Whelan, the *Oral History Project* would have floundered long ago.

The significance of Whelan's contribution (along with Grothier and Mac Conmara) must not be underestimated. The latter half of the twentieth century has seen a shift in archival thought and professional practice, away from seeing the archive as a monolith of bureaucratic evidence forming a singular, official state narrative, to viewing it as a contested space, characterised by competing narratives, with some dominant and others subdued, suppressed or hidden. The attempts by de Valera to establish an archive from the anti-Treaty perspective, and the various biases discernible in the Military Archives in its formative years, discussed in an earlier chapter, are practical examples of this. The job of the contemporary archivist is to ensure that diverse narratives find their way faithfully into the Archive, and it behoves the profession, where a particular narrative, or the experiences of an individual or group, has been ignored or suppressed or simply missed, that this is addressed and balanced. Such instances do not have to be overtly dramatic, malicious or even deliberate. In the case of the Defence Forces, it is a natural consequence of being a rigidly hierarchically structured organisation that the majority of administrative documentation is generated by those holding high rank. More than anyone, Whelan has shaped an *Oral History Project* that captures a much more representative cross-section of knowledge and experience for posterity, filling in the gaps in memory and experience that official records alone cannot.

Archives are often institutions based around discourses of power and authority, but they also have the capacity to accommodate narratives that have little to do with the original purpose of the institution. One of the most unexpected collections to be deposited with the Military Archives in recent years is that of Uinseann Mac Eoin.

Uinseann Ó Rathaille Mac Eoin was, among many other things, a veteran republican activist, architect and town planner, journalist, and campaigner for the conservation of Georgian built heritage. As a historian, Mac Eoin published three books: *Survivors* (1980) which documents the story of the struggle for Irish independence as told through interviews with veteran republicans; *Harry* (1985) the biography of IRA man Harry White; and *The IRA in the Twilight Years 1923–1948* (1997), which tells the story of the IRA between the period 1923–1948. Mac Eoin's books, naturally, drew very much on the republican tradition, and for a long time he would have been 'persona non grata' in Irish Defence Forces installations. Mac Eoin was jailed for a year for IRA membership and interned during the Emergency.

As part of his research and publishing work, he amassed 102 audio cassette recordings of interviews that he conducted from the late 1970s until the early 1990s with veteran Irish republicans about their activities from the 1920s to the 1940s, as well as nine boxes of associated paperwork and photographs. Mac Eoin died in 2007 and in 2016 his family, on the recommendation of Professor Diarmaid Ferriter, deposited the material with the Military Archives.

In 2019, the release of this collection formed the theme of the Archives' Christmas Coffee Morning. For these archives of a self-described 'sulphurous old Fenian' to be deposited at the Military Archives, and to have the Chief of Staff of the Defence Forces address the gathered attendees, symbolised both 'a dividend of the Peace Process' (as his daughter Aoife described it) and the mature and confident institution that the Military Archives had become. Upon being asked how his father would have felt about it, his son Nuada suggested that the irony would have appealed to his particular sense of humour. It was a most significant accession. As the Officer-in-Charge declared during his address that morning, 'there is no such thing as too many sources.'

***

As the Military Archives approaches its second century, it still faces challenges. The Defence Forces is significantly under-strength, with serious difficulties in recruiting and retaining personnel. This has naturally had knock-on effects for the Archives in the provision of certain necessary support and infrastructural services. There is also the incongruence with the essential requirement of Officers-in-Charge of the Military

Archives to nurture relationships, establish networks and develop corporate memory, and what are traditionally considered the norms and requirements of military officers' career paths, characterised by constantly changing appointments and chasing promotions. The Military Archives is a unique entity within the Defence Forces. It has had only six, fully qualified archivists hold the appointment of Officer-in-Charge since 1982. The usual rotation for officers in other military staff sections is two to three years. The Military Archives is also the most publicly facing and publicly engaging section in the Defence Forces, more so even than the Press Office. The absence of formal processes to guarantee the retention of corporate memory and capacity for officers and NCOs who are qualified and interested to be given certainty of long-term appointments makes the prospect of the future civilianisation a potential threat in the long term.

That said, ever since it was established, with the exception of the past decade, the very existence of the Military Archives has been one of enduring neglect (by elements within both the Defence Forces and Department of Defence) and scarcity of resources. It now enjoys the support of the Defence Forces, the Department of Defence and Government generally, and can hold its own operating alongside any other heritage institution at home or abroad. The Military Archives has been built, over the past century, on the work of its military and civilian staff for whom it has been, and remains, a labour of love. It now stands in the best position it ever has, to pursue its purpose as it was eloquently and succinctly described by 'the Father of the Military Archives', Commandant Peter Young:

To protect the past, to understand the present, and to plan for the future.

NOTES

Foreword

1   From the citation to former OiC
    Military Archives Commandant
    Victor Laing on the occasion of his
    being awarded an honorary doctorate
    by University College Dublin for
    his career-defining work developing
    Military Archives.

Prologue

1   Military Service (1916-1923) Pensions
    Collection, W24SP295, W24E3.

2   Military Service (1916-1923) Pensions
    Collection, W24SP5367, W24B833;
    Bureau of Military History WS 1758;
    O/182 Capt JJ Burke Personal File.

3   Department of Defence 'A/'
    Files, *Memo from Piaras Béaslaí*,
    Commandant General P Béaslaí
    Personal File, IE/MA/A/11672.

4   Piarais Béaslaí Papers, National
    Library of Ireland, Ms 33,913(15).

5   The Military Secretary Papers, *Letter
    from Commandant General Piaras
    Béaslaí to the Chief of General Staff*, 20
    June 1923, IE/MA/MS161.

6   Piarais Béaslaí Papers,
    National Library of Ireland,
    Ms 33,913(15).

7   The Military Secretary Papers,
    *Letter from the Military Secretary to
    Commandant General Piaras Béaslaí*, 2
    July 1923, IE/MA/MS161.

8   Piarais Béaslaí Papers, National
    Library of Ireland, Ms 33,913(15).

9   Department of Defence 'A/' Files,
    *Memo from the President's Office to
    Michael McDunphy*, Commandant
    General P Béaslaí Personal File, IE/
    MA/A/11672.

10 Béaslaí, Piarais. 1930. *Michael Collins
    and the Making of a New Ireland
    (Popular Edition)*. Vol 1. Dublin:
    Phoenix: ix-x.

11 Ibid.: xi.

12 Hart, Peter, *Book Review: Michael
    Collins and the making of a new Ireland
    (2 vols)*, History Ireland, March / April
    2010, https://www.historyireland.com/
    michael-collins-and-the-making-of-a-
    new-ireland-2-vols

13 Maume, Patrick, *Piaras Béaslaí*,
    Dictionary of Irish Biography, RIA.

Chapter 1

1   Military Secretary Papers, *Organisation
    – Intelligence Branch, 1924*, IE/MA/
    MS/9/10.

2   History of the Military Archives, *Historical Documents and the Formation of Military Archives,* 2 December 1924, IE/MA/HMA.

3   The Chief-of Staff's Branch at that time consisted of: The Chief of Staff himself, the Chief Staff Officer's Branch, the Military Secretarial Branch, the Training and Operations Branch, the Intelligence Branch, and the Staff Duties Branch. Defence Forces Regulations: Defence Forces (Organisation) Order, 1924.

4   Army Inquiry Committee (1924) Papers, *Verbatim Report of Evidence of Witness, Colonel Charles Russell,* 10 May 1924, IE/MA/AMTY/03/036.

5   History of the Military Archives, *Letter from Colonel MJ Costello to the Chief of Staff,* 2 December 1924, IE/MA/HMA.

6   Captain Alphonsus Blake Personal File, *Letter from Major General Michael Brennan to Peter Hughes, Minister for Defence,* 3 February 1927.

7   History of the Military Archives, *Draft of Proposed Establishment by Thomas Galvin,* 11 February 1925, IE/MA/HMA

8   O'Brien, Gerard, *Irish Government and the Guardianship of Historical Records, 1922-1972* (Dublin: Four Courts Press, 2004), 11.

9   Béaslaí, Piarais, *Michael Collins and the Making of a New Ireland (Popular Edition).* Vol 1. (Dublin: Phoenix, 1930), xi.

10 O'Brien, *Irish Government and the Guardianship of Historical Records,* p. 16.

11 History of Military Archives, *Memorandum from Captain NC Harrington to the Director of No.2 Bureau,* 25 June 1930, IE/MA/HMA.

12 Chief Secretary's Office Papers, National Archives of Ireland, *Thomas Markham to Sir Philip Hanson, Commissioner of Public Works,* 4 July 1924, CSO/3/719/4.

13 *Irish Times, Novel Castle Incident,* 9 Jan 1925.

14 History of Military Archives, *Letter from Commandant WJ Brennan Whitmore to Colonel MJ Costello,* 20 February 1925, IE/MA/HMA.

15 History of Military Archives, *Letter from Chief of Staff to Minister for Defence,* 30 March 1925, IE/MA/HMA.

16 History of Military Archives, *Letter from Director of Intelligence to the Chief of Staff,* 16 April 1925, IE/MA/HMA.

17 History of Military Archives, *Letter from Chief of Staff to Minister for Defence,* 3 June 1925, IE/MA/HMA.

18 History of Military Archives, *Letter from Chief of Staff to Minister for Defence,* 16 November 1925, IE/MA/HMA.

19 History of Military Archives, *Memo from Assistant Chief of Staff to Minister for Defence,* 24 November 1925, and reply from CB O'Connor, 26 November 1925, IE/MA/HMA.

20 Council of Defence Records, *Minutes of the Meeting of the Council of Defence,* 14 Dec 1925, IE/MA/COD/2.

21 History of Military Archives, *Memorandum on the Military Archives,* Captain Niall Charles Harrington, 25 June 1930, IE/MA/HMA.

22 Council of Defence Records, *Letter from Commissioner of Public Works to Secretary of Department of Defence,* 25 Jul 1925, IE/MA/COD/01.

23 Council of Defence Records, *Minutes of the Meeting of the Council of Defence*, 22 Oct 1926, IE/MA/COD/2.

24 McCullagh, David. 2017. *De Valera: Rise 1882-1932*. Vol. 1. Dublin: Gill Books: 333.

25 Ibid., 338.

26 Ibid., 413.

27 Ibid., 335.

28 Ibid., 338.

29 Ibid., 351.

30 History of Military Archives, *Raid on Pierce Beasley's Premises for Documents*, Eastern Command Intelligence Officer to Director of Intelligence, 22 October 1925, IE/MA/HMA.

31 Bureau of Military History, *Witness Statement of JJ O'Kelly (Skeilg)*, WS384.

32 Cook, Terry, 'Evidence, Memory, Identity and Community: Four Shifting Archives Paradigms', *Archival Science* 13: 95 (2013).

33 Ibid., 108.

34 For example, the work of people like Anne Gilliland, Alan Flinn, Sue McKemmish and Elizabeth Shepherd is typically illustrative of these currents in contemporary archival academia.

35 McKemmish, Sue, and Anne Gilliland. 2001. 'Archival Recordkeeping Research: Past, Present and Future,' Chap. 4 in Williamson, Kevin and Johanson, Graeme, *Research Methods: Information, Systems, and Contexts* (Prahan, Victoria: Tilde University Press), 84.

36 Ibid., 86.

37 Caswell, Michelle, and Anne Gilliland, 'False Promise and New Hope: Dead Perpetrators, Imagined Documents and Emergent Archival Evidence', T*he International Journal of Human Rights* 19:5 (2015).

38 Gilliland, Anne, 'Moving Past: Probing the Agency and Affect of Recordkeeping in Individual and Community Lives in Post-Conflict Croatia' *Archival Science* 14:3 (2014), 261.

39 Morrison, Eve. 2011. PhD Dissertation: The Bureau of Military History: A Separatist Veteran's Narrative of the Irish Revolution. Dublin: TCD.

40 Historical Section Collection, *Memorandum on the General Staff*, Thomas Galvin, 31 October 1925, IE/MA/HS/A/025.

41 Historical Section Collection, *Letter from Mr Michael McDunphy to Major Ryan, Office of Adjutant General*, 1 December 1925, IE/MA/HS/A/025.

42 Council of Defence Records, *Memorandum for the Council of Defence: Civilian Clerks and Typists – Establishments*, 9 Sep 1925, IE/MA/COD/01.

43 History of the Military Archives, *Report from Thomas Galvin to Captain A Blake*, 8 December 1925, IE/MA/HMA.

44 History of the Military Archives, *Letter from Assistant Chief of Staff to Minister for Defence*, 25 May 1926, IE/MA/HMA.

45 O/079 Captain Alphonsus Blake, Personal File.

46 History of the Military Archives, *Letter from the Chief of Staff to the Minister for Defence*, 25 May 1926, IE/MA/HMA.

Chapter 2

1 The six principal members of the Mission were Major General Hugh MacNeill, Colonel Michael Costello, Major Joseph Dunne, Captain Patrick

Berry, Lieutenant Seán Collins-Powell and 2nd Lieutenant Charles Trodden.

2 The full duties of these sections were as follows:

Section 'A': Internal Espionage. Collection, evaluation and distribution of information, in cooperation with other Government intelligence agencies, of information relating to: -
  (i) Anti-State movements.
  (ii) Unauthorised military organisations.
  (iii) Secret societies.
  (iv) Communists.
  (v) Disloyal elements in the Army.
  And all other potential hostile influences or agencies.

Section 'B': Topographical and Statistical.
  (i) Topographical and statistical matters.
  (ii) Field intelligence duties.

Section 'C': Publicity.
  (i) Press relations.
  (ii) Publicity.
  (iii) Press censorship in time of war.
  (iv) An tÓglách.

Section 'D': Foreign Armies.
  (i) Collection and distribution of information re foreign armies.
  (ii) Development in sciences of war.
  (iii) Technical information, inventions, armaments, production and movements.
  (iv) Military reference libraries.

3 The Army Crisis, also known as the Army Mutiny, took place in 1924 when a group within the Army, known as the IRA Organisation (IRAO), with the support of a faction within government led by the Minister for Labour, Joe McGrath, issued an ultimatum to the government "to suspend, and establish an enquiry into, demobilisation and reorganisation and to give the IRAO a say in it."

4 *Report of the Army Organisation Board 1925-1926*, IE/MA/Army Organisation Board.

5 The Report of the Army Organisation Board recommended that the duties of the General Staff be broken down into three parts:
  The Directorate, headed by the Assistant Chief of Staff with the Chief Staff Officer as his immediate assistant;
  The (1st) Training Bureau, responsible for all training, schools and physical culture, and;
  The (2nd) Intelligence Bureau.
In two- or three-years' time, the Board suggested, the Army could be in a position to introduce a staff structure based on 4 bureaus similar to the American or French models at that time. This would see the Army staff organised as follows:
  1st Bureau: Personnel – corresponding to the Branch of the Adjutant General;
  2nd Bureau: Training – corresponding to the Training Bureau of the General Staff;
  3rd Bureau: Intelligence – corresponding to the Intelligence Bureau of the General Staff, and; 4th Bureau: Supply – corresponding to the Branch of the Quartermaster General.

6 Location and Strength Reports, *Confidential Report for month ending 31st January 1927*, IE/MA/LS/Box 21.

7   Council of Defence Records, *Agenda for Council of Defence Meeting 9 May 1927*, IE/MA/COD/03.

8   Location and Strength Reports, *Confidential Report for month ending 28th February 1927*, IE/MA/LS/Box 21.

9   Location and Strength Reports, *Confidential Report for Quarter ending 30th September 1927*, IE/MA/LS/Box 21.

10   Location and Strength Reports, *Confidential Report for Quarter ending 31st December 1928*, IE/MA/LS/Box 21.

11   Location and Strength Reports, *Confidential Report for Quarter ending 31st March 1929*, IE/MA/LS/Box 21.

12   History of Military Archives, *Correspondence between the Chief Staff Officer and Director of Intelligence, 22 November, 12 December, 20 December 1928*, IE/MA/HMA.

13   Location and Strength Reports, *Report for the Month of October, 1929*, Colonel J.J. O'Connell to Chief of Staff, 1 November 1929, IE/MA/LS/Box 21.

14   Location and Strength Reports, *Report for the Month of November, 1929*, Colonel J.J. O'Connell to Chief of Staff, 6 December 1929, IE/MA/LS/Box 21.

15   Location and Strength Reports, *Confidential Report on the Work of Number 2 Bureau from October 1st 1929, to March 31st 1930*, Colonel J.J. O'Connell to Chief of Staff, 4 April 1930, IE/MA/LS/Box 21.

16   Historical Section Records, *Letter from Colonel J.J. O'Connell to Chief Staff Officer*, 1 July 1930, IE/MA/HS/A/841.

17   Historical Section Records, *Minute sheet containing directions of the Chief of Staff, 3 May 1930*, IE/MA/HS/A/841.

18   *Civil War Operations Reports*, IE/MA/CW/OPS.

19   Historical Section Records, *Letter from Colonel J.J. O'Connell to Chief Staff Officer*, 1 July 1930, IE/MA/HS/A/841.

20   Historical Section Records: See IE/MA/HS/413 and IE/MA/HS/622.

21   Location and Strength Reports, *Half Yearly Report*, Colonel J.J. O'Connell to Chief of Staff, 27 October 1930, IE/MA/LS/Box 21.

22   Location and Strength Reports, *Confidential Half-Yearly Report*, Colonel J.J. O'Connell to Chief of Staff, 22 April 1932, IE/MA/LS/Box 21.

23   Military Service (1916-1923) Pensions Collection, *Destruction of Records*, DOD/2012/1.

Chapter 3

1   Duggan, J.P. *A History of the Irish Army* (Dublin: Gill and Macmillan, 1991), 144.

2   Major General E.V. O'Carroll Personal File, *Letter from Officer Commanding St. Bricin's Hospital to the Director of Medical Services*, 26 August 1926.

3   Military Service (1916-1923) Pensions Collection, 24SP3706, 24D77.

4   Major General E.V. O'Carroll Personal File, *Annual Performance Report 1928*.

5   Ferriter, Diarmaid. 'in such deadly ernest', *The Dublin Review*, No.12 (Autumn 2003).

6   O'Halpin, Eunan. *Defending Ireland: The Irish State and its Enemies since 1922* (Oxford: OUP, 1999), 98-102.

7   Morrison, Eve, 'Bureau of Military History witness statements as sources for the Irish Revolution', *Bureau of Military History Contextualising Essays* (2002): 2. Could you insert a website address? https://www.militaryarchives.ie/

collections/online-collections/
bureau-of-military-history-1913-1921/
wp-content/uploads/2019/06/
Bureau_of_Military_witness_state-
ments-as_sources-for_the_Irish-
Revolution.pdf

8   Zinn, Howard, 'Secrecy, Archives and
the Public Interest', *The Midwestern
Archivist* 2:2 (1977), 14-26.

9   Historical Section Records, *Letter from
Colonel E.V. O'Carroll to Major General
Michael Brennan*, 31 October 1933, IE/
MA/HS/001(iv).

10   Historical Section Records, *Leathán
Miontuairisce [Briefing Sheet] from
Major General Michael Brennan to
Colonel E.V. O'Carroll*, 31 October
1933, IE/MA/HS/001(iv)

11   Historical Section Records, *Letter from
Colonel E.V. O'Carroll to Officer-in-
Charge of Personnel*, 8 November 1933,
IE/MA/HS/001(i).

12   Young, Peter, 'Military Archives in
the Defence Forces', *An Cosantóir*
(September, 1977).

13   Young, Peter, 'Military Archives, The
First Year', *An Cosantóir* (October,
1983).

14   Historical Section Records, *Circular
Letter from Colonel E.V. O'Carroll*, 15
January 1934, MA/HS/A/001(iii).

15   Historical Section Records, *Anglo-Irish
Conflict History 1913-1921. General
Correspondence: Regular Officers*, MA/
HS/A/001(iii).

16   Ibid.

17   Ibid.

18   Ibid.

19   Ibid.

20   Ibid.

21   Ibid.

22   Ibid.

23   Ibid.

24   Ibid.

25   Ibid.

26   Bureau of Military History,
Witness Statement of Liam Daly,
WS425.

27   Historical Section Records, *Circular
Letter from Colonel E.V. O'Carroll*, 5
April 1934, IE/MA/HS/A/001(iv).

28   National Library of Ireland, *MS
10915/1-16*.

29   Historical Section Records, *Letter
from Colonel E.V. O'Carroll to Chief
of Staff*, 17 April 1934, IE/MA/
HS/A/001(iv).

30   Historical Section Records, *Circular
Letter from Chief of Staff*, April 1934,
IE/MA/HS/A/001(ii).

31   Historical Section Records, *Anglo-Irish
Conflict History 1913-1921. General
Correspondence: Regular Officers*, MA/
HS/A/001(iii).

32   Historical Section Records, *Letter from
Captain N.C. Harrington to Denis
Begley*, 13 September 1935, IE/MA/
HS/A/001(vii).

Chapter 4

1   Ó Corráin, Daithí, 'J.J. O'Connell's
Memoir of the Irish Volunteers, 1914-
17', *Analecta Hibernica*, 47 (2016), 1.

2   Bureau of Military History, *Witness
Statement of Josephine MacNeill*,
WS303.

3   Coogan, Tim Pat, *De Valera: Long
Fellow, Long Shadow* (London: Arrow,
1993:, 255-279.

4   Fewer, Michael, *The Battle of the Four
Courts* (London: Head of Zeus),
68-69. **2018.**

5   Coogan, Tim Pat, *Michael Collins*
(London: Arrow), 330-331. **1991.**

6   Dorney, John, *The Civil War in Dublin: The Fight for the Irish Capital* (Dublin: Irish Academic Press) 67. **2017.**

7   Ibid., 235.

8   In November 1922, as part of the Army's reorganisation during the Civil War, Commander-in-Chief and Minister for Defence Richard Mulcahy replaced Liam Tobin with Diarmuid O'Hegarty as Director of Intelligence, and moved the directorate out of Wellington Barracks and into their new headquarters at Parkgate Street. This reorganisation was driven by ill-discipline and poor training within the National Army, understandable given that it had only months ago formed from a mix of guerrilla fighters and former British soldiers, but Army Intelligence was of particular concern to Mulcahy. This was because it was comprised of many former Squad men and had become a law unto themselves, with their ill-discipline going as far as summary executions.

9   JJ O'Connell Papers, National Library of Ireland, *Letter from Mary Margaret Pegeen to Niamh O'Connell*, 23 November 1950, MS 22,158.

10   McCullagh, David, *De Valera: Rise 1882-1932*. Vol. 1. (Dublin: Gill Books, 2017), 80.

11   Colonel JJ O'Connell Personal File, *Annual Confidential Report 1935.*

12   Colonel JJ O'Connell Personal File, *Letter from Colonel JJ O'Connell to the Chief of Staff*, 15 March 1927.

13   Colonel JJ O'Connell Personal File, *Annual Confidential Report 1927-1928*, 3 July 1928.

14   Colonel JJ O'Connell Personal File, *Annual Confidential Report 1929-1930*, 19 May 1930.

15   Lieutenant Colonel NC Harrington Personal File, *Annual Confidential Report 1929-1930*, April 1930.

16   Historical Section Records, *Military Archives Locations and Duties*, IE/MA/HS/A/004.

17   Ibid.

18   Historical Section Records, *Letter from Colonel JJ O'Connell to Chief of Staff*, 12 June 1935, IE/MA/HS/A/001(iv).

19   Historical Section Records, *Letter from Chief of Staff to Colonel JJ O'Connell*, 13 June 1935, IE/MA/HS/A/001(iv).

20   Historical Section Records, *Letter from Colonel JJ O'Connell to Chief of Staff*, 14 June 1935, IE/MA/HS/A/001(iv).

21   Historical Section Records, *Letter from Colonel JJ O'Connell to Chief of Staff*, 8 November 1935, IE/MA/HS/004.

22   Historical Section Records, *Letter from WP Blunden to Colonel JJ O'Connell*, 18 November 1935, IE/MA/HS/004.

23   69810 Corporal Gerard Deignan, Personal File.

24   O'Halpin, Eunan. *Defending Ireland: The Irish State and its Enemies since 1922* (Oxford: OUP, 1999), 352.

25   Historical Section Records, *Letter from Colonel JJ O'Connell to Chief of Staff*, 21 October 1936, IE/MA/HS/A/010.

26   Historical Section Records, *Letter from Colonel JJ O'Connell to Colonel Liam Archer*, 4 February 1937, IE/MA/HS/A/010.

27   Historical Section Records, *Letter from Colonel JJ O'Connell to Chief of Staff*, 24 August 1936, IE/MA/HS/004.

28   Historical Section Records, *Letter from Colonel JJ O'Connell to Assistant*

Chief of Staff, 11 January 1936, IE/MA/HS/A/41.

29   Historical Section Records, *Na Fianna: Origin and History*, 1936, IE/MA/HS/A/41.

30   Historical Section Records, *Ulster Volunteers*, [1936], IE/MA/HS/A/48.

31   Historical Section Records, *Letter from Colonel JJ O'Connell to Chief of Staff*, 25 June 1935, IE/MA/HS/A/001(iv).

32   Historical Section Records, *Letter from Captain Sean O'Neill to Colonel JJ. O'Carroll*, 18 November 1935, IE/MA/HS/004.

33   Historical Section Records, *Letter from Colonel JJ O'Connell to Dr. Kiernan*, 3 January 1936, IE/MA/HS/003.

34   Historical Section Records, *Letter from Colonel JJ O'Connell to Mr. Noel Harnett*, 13 January 1936, IE/MA/HS/003.

35   Historical Section Records, *Letter from Sir Henry McAnally to Colonel JJ O'Connell*, 4 May 1936, IE/MA/HS/003.

36   Historical Section Records, *Letter from Sir Henry McAnally to Colonel JJ O'Connell*, 8 May 1936, IE/MA/HS/003.

37   Colonel JJ O'Connell Personal File, *Annual Confidential Report 1942-1943*.

38   The Chief of Staff's Report to the Minister for Defence for year 1st April 1946 to 31st March 1947.

39   The Chief of Staff's Report to the Minister for Defence for year 1st April 1948 to 31st March 1949.

40   Colonel Dan Bryan, *Care of Historical Documents (circular)*, 1948, IE/MA/COS/1696.

41   *Memorandum for the Government: Reorganisation of the Defence Forces, 1958*, July 1958.

42   Director of Intelligence to Chief of Staff, 4th October 1971, IE/MA/COS/1696.

Chapter 5

1   Fisk, Robert, Phone Interview with Commandant Daniel Ayiotis, 26 and 28 February 2019.

2   In parliamentary questions on 14 Feb 1975, James Kilfedder asked the Secretary of State for Foreign and Commonwealth Affairs (1) on whose instructions, and for what purpose, Mr. Robert Fisk, Belfast correspondent of The Times, was questioned by a member of the staff of the British Embassy in Dublin; who was present with the official; and if he will ensure that officials of British embassies in foreign countries make clear to British subjects whom they are questioning the reasons for the questions; (2) what is the nationality of the member of the staff of the British Embassy in Dublin who interviewed Mr. Robert Fisk; how long he has been a member of the staff at that embassy; and what are his rank and duties. The reply was that Daly was Head of Chancery of the British Embassy in Dublin, who is a British subject and an established member of Her Majesty's Diplomatic Service. The report of this UK parliamentary debate can be found at: https://hansard.parliament.uk/Commons/1975-02-14/debates/fd38583a-eda2-44bb-b545-997fece84049/MrRobertFisk?highlight=robert%20fisk#contribution-cb7e2879-ef76-4784-b4c5-cf75ae557faf

3   O'Donnell, Commandant PD. "How to Research a Barrack History." *An Cosantóir* (September 1977).

4   Young, Captain Peter. "Military Archives in the Defence Forces." *An Cosantóir* (September 1977).

5   Directorate of Planning and Research, PR1 Proposals, 30 September 1980.

6   Directorate of Training Memo, *Proposed Establishment of Military Archives,* 11 August 1980.

7   Archives Sub-Section Files. *Letter from Commandant Peter Young to Director of Intelligence,* 8 March 1982, G2/L/17.

8   Young, Commandant Peter. "Military Archives – The First Year." *An Cosantóir,* October 1983.

9   Niall Charles Harrington Papers, National Library of Ireland. *Letter from Commandant Peter Young to Mrs Nuala Jordan,* 25 October 1983, MSS 40,614-40,999.

10   Section 8, 4, (a)-(c) of the National Archives of Ireland Act, 1986, permits for records over thirty years of age to be withheld from public inspection in cases where to do so would: not be in the public interest; constitute a breach of statutory duty; or cause serious distress or danger to living people. Closure certificates must be made by an appointed departmental *Certifying Officer* and approved by a *Consenting Officer* of the Department of An Taoiseach. Once granted, these closures must be reviewed every five years.

11   The Bodkin Report had been commissioned by the 1948-51 Inter Party Government and led ultimately to the founding of The Arts Council.

12   Department of Defence letter and attached memorandum, ref 3/10093, 11 August 1978, G2/L/17.

13   Letter from AT Lucas, Director of the National Museum of Ireland, to the Secretary, Department of Education, 21 September 1973, G2/L/17.

14   The committee consisted of: Dr Joseph Rafferty (Director of the National Museum of Ireland); Mr C O'Reilly and Mr M O'Donoghue of the Department of Defence; and Colonel P Daly, Lieutenant Colonel M Fitzsimons, Commandant F O'Donovan and Commandant N Heffernan of the Defence Forces.

15   Letter from Commandant Peter Young to Officer-in-Charge Accommodation, Barrack Services Section, 14 June 1982, G2/L/17.

16   Letter from Frank W Harte Architect to Quartermaster General, 24 September 1982, G2/L/17.

17   Letter from Commandant Peter Young to Officer-in-Charge Barrack Services Section, 22 November 1982. G2/L/17.

18   Letter from Lieutenant Colonel Con Costello, Chairman, Museum Committee, 26 April 1983, G2/L/17.

19   Draft reply from Minister for Defence to unattributed recipient, [1985], G2/L/17.

20   Colonel DJ Coffey, Command and Staff Course Assessment of Commandant Peter Young, 27 August 1991.

21   Letter from Commandant Peter Young to Director of Intelligence, 29 August 1990, G2/L/17.

22   Dáil Éireann Debate, Wednesday, 13 Jun 1990, Vol. 399, No. 11.

Chapter 6

1   Letter from Edward F Gormley to the Chief of Staff, 6 May 1991, G2/L/17.

2   McCarthy, Patrick, Interview with Commandant Daniel Ayiotis, The Military Archives, 22 March 2021.

3   Letter from Mr Justice Niall McCarthy to the Minister for Defence, 26 March 1991, G2/L/17.

4   Letter from Lieutenant Colonel John Duggan, Director of Intelligence, to Chief of Staff, 14 May 1991, G2/L/17.

5   McCarthy, Denis. "Information… Information…" *An Cosantóir,* November/December 1988. This article gives an entertaining but detailed introduction to McCarthy's involvement with the Military Archives and its use of information technology. It is highly recommended reading for both its humorous style and the fact that McCarthy has been a volunteer at the Military Archives for over thirty years.

6   In September 1985, an Irish Government white paper made each department responsible for its information technology strategy and revised the mandate of the Central Data Processing Service (CDPS) mainframe bureau in Kilmainham. Under a new name, the Central Computer Service (CCS), its role would be to provide processing to departments and offices that could not support its own systems and operations.

7   Letter from Commandant Peter Young to Director of Intelligence, 2 August 1990, G2/L/17.

8   Letter from Denis McCarthy to Minister for Defence, 14 May 1990, G2/L/17.

9   Letter from Denis McCarthy to Minister for Defence, 10 August 1993, G2/L/17.

10 Denis, if you're reading this, I've no doubt it was attrition!

11 Letter from Colonel P Keogh, Director of Intelligence, to Commandant Peter Young, 24 June 1992.

12 McCarthy, Patrick, Interview with Commandant Daniel Ayiotis, The Military Archives, 22 March 2021.

13 These witness statements and accompanying documents, collected during the 1940s-1950s from persons who took part in military activities during the 1913-1921, were held in a strongroom in the Taoiseach's Department. In 1999, as Young anticipated, they were released to the custody of the Military Archives.

14 Minutes of Meeting, National Museum and Defence Forces Museum Board, McKee Barracks, 31 May 1994.

15 Dáil Éireann Debates, Thursday, 18 May 1995, Vol. 453, No. 2 and Tuesday, 17 Oct 1995, Vol. 457 No. 1.

16 Minutes of Meeting, National Museum, Defence Forces and Museum Consultants, 16 January 1997.

17 Seanad Éireann Debate, Wednesday, 26 May 1999, Vol. 159, No. 12.

18 I'm afraid I can't divulge this source, you'll have to take my word!

19 *Evening Echo*, Tuesday, March 26, 1996.

20 Commandant Peter Young Obituary, *Irish Times*, 13 November 1999.

21 Report from Commandant Peter Young to Mr B Coghlan, Department of Defence, 7 September 1994.

22 Bureau of Military History, Director's Report, 1957.

23 Morrison, Eve, 'The Bureau of Military History,' in Crowley, J, O Drisceoil, D. Murphy, M. Borgonovo, J. (eds), *The Atlas of the Irish Revolution* (Cork: Cork University Press, 2017), 876-880.

24 Crowe, Catriona, Interview with Commandant Daniel Ayiotis, The Military Archives, 12 April 2019.

25 Crowe, Catriona, Interview with Commandant Daniel Ayiotis, The Military Archives, 12 April 2019.

26 Letter from Assistant Chief of Staff to Director of Intelligence, 6 March 1997.

Chapter 7

1 Dáil Éireann debate, Tuesday, 10 Dec 2002, Vol. 559 No. 1.

2 Section 8 (4) (a)-(c) of the National Archives of Ireland Act, 1986, allows for records over thirty years old to be withheld from public inspection where to do so: would be contrary to the public interest; would or might constitute a breach of statutory duty, or a breach of good faith on the ground that they contain information supplied in confidence; would or might cause distress or danger to living persons on the ground that they contain information about individuals, or would or might be likely to lead to an action for damages for defamation.

3 Crowe, Catriona, Interview with Commandant Daniel Ayiotis, The Military Archives, 12 April 2019.

4 Report on Interdepartmental Committee Meeting held 28 May 2004, Commandant Laing to Chief of Staff, Lieutenant General Dermot Earley, 1 June 2004.

5 Dáil Éireann Debate, Tuesday, 9 May 2006, Vol. 619, No. 1.

6 Campbell, Commandant Billy, Interview with Commandant Daniel Ayiotis, The Military Archives, 25 March 2021.

7 Minister Alan Shatter TD in Crowe, Catriona, ed. 2012. *Guide to the Military Service (1916-1923) Pensions*

Collection. Dublin: Irish Defence Forces.

8 Dáil Éireann Debate, Wednesday, 6 May 2009, Vol. 681, No. 4.

9 Seanad Éireann Debate, Friday, 10 Jul 2009, Vol. 196 No. 14.

10 Dáil Éireann Debate, Wednesday, 8 Dec 2010, Vol. 724 No. 2.

11 Dáil Éireann Debate, Tuesday, 7 Jun 2011, Vol. 734 No. 3.

12 Dáil Éireann debate, Tuesday, 17 Jan 2012, Vol. 751 No. 4.

13 Dáil Éireann debate, Tuesday 19 June 2012, Vol. 769 No.1.

14 This board was consisted of Colonel B Reade (President), Brigitta O'Doherty (Department of Defence), Lieutenant Colonel P Kelly, Lieutenant Colonel B Hume, Commandant Victor Laing, Commandant F McCarthy and Captain S Mac Eoin. Catriona Crowe (National Archives) was Special Consultant to the Board.

15 Report of the Defence Forces Board Assembled to Examine Military Archives, July 2011, *Executive Summary*, p.7.

16 Ibid., p.32.

Chapter 8

1 Kennedy, Lieutenant Colonel Padraic, Interview with Commandant Daniel Ayiotis, The Military Archives, 27 April 2021.

2 The Irish Defence Forces participated in the UNAMET/UNTAET missions to East Timor between July 1999 and May 2004.

3 The Military Archives uniform collection stands at approximately 300 uniforms as well as accoutrements

and accessories, ranging from the period of the Irish Volunteers until the present day. The cataloguing project is managed by volunteer Flight Sergeant James Perkins (retired).

4 This was recommended by the *Report of the Defence Forces Board Assembled to Examine Military Archives, June 2011*.

5 Dáil Éireann Debates, Tuesday, 5 Mar 2013 Vol. 795 No. 1, and Wednesday, 8 May 2013, Vol. 802 No. 2.

6 Seanad Éireann Debate, Wednesday, 10 Dec 2014, Vol. 236 No. 4.

7 Áras an Uachtaráin YouTube Channel, *President Michael D Higgins opened the new Military Archives building in Cathal Brugha Barracks, Rathmines*, www.youtube.com/watch?v=mknEO-QfGaIw&t=122s

8 Higgins, President Michael D, *Speech Marking the Official Opening of the Military Archives*, Cathal Brugha Barracks, 26 April 2016.

INDEX

Act of Union 11

Adams, Gerry 148

Ahern, Bertie 137

Air Corps Museum 154

Ancient Order of Hibernians 80

Anderson, John 10

Andrews, David 117–118

Angliss, Henry James 55

Anglo-Irish Conflict (1913–1921) Project 28, 44–46, 56, 74

Anglo-Irish War of Independence 2, 10

Anglo-Irish Treaty 10, 49, 59

Anti-Treaty Archive 21–27, 155

Arbour Hill Prison 22

Archer, Liam 40–41, 50, 55

Army Crisis 2, 33

Army Enquiry Committee 2, 17, 20, 61

Army Equitation School 40

Army Medical Service 50

Army and Military Service Pensions Acts 33

Army Mutiny 3, 17, 20

Army Organisation Board (1925-1926) 33, 74

Army Pensions Act (1923) 1

Army Pensions Bill (1927) 34

Army Pensions Board 34

Army School of Instruction 63

Artillery Barracks Kildare 49

Ayiotis, Daniel 152

Ballykinlar 139

Barrett, Seán 121, 135

Béaslaí, Piaras 1, 7, 22, 74

   raid on home 23

Beckett, Hugh 137

Beggars Bush Barracks 49

Begley, Denis 55

Belleek RIC Barracks 49

Blackwater Manoeuvres 86

Blake, Alphonsus 5, 22

   resignation 31

Blunden, W.P. 68

Bodkin Report on the Arts in Ireland 99

Braveheart 124, 130

   unfulfilled promises to Irish Defence Forces 124–125

Brennan, Michael 5–6, 63

Brennan, Pat 131, 135, 137, 153

Brennan-Whitmore, William James 16–17, 23

British Museum 13

Brother Allen Collection 154

Brugha, Cathal 60

Bruton, Richard 139

Bryan, Dan 39, 81–83, 99, 104, 126

Bureau of Military History (1913–1921) 13, 27, 45, 52, 125–128

   accommodation needs 121

   establishment of 80, 126

online 143–144, 146
release 133
scope 126
secure storage 127
Witness Statements 58
'Burn Order' 12, 40, 109
see also Destruction Order
Byrne, Eric J. 107
Byrne, Kevin 152
Byrne, William 52

Calendar of State Papers 10
Callaghan, William 'Bull' 92
Campbell, Billy 136
Carbery, Deirdre 146
Castle Papers 9, 19
Castlereagh Holding Centre 89
Cathal Brugha Barracks 85, 95, 106, 107, 113,
    133, 134
    hospital block refurbishment 142
Chadwicke, Michael 23
Chemin, Cécile 137, 153
Civil War Intelligence and Operations Records
    4
Coast Watching Service 97
Cohmairle na dTeachtaí 22
Colbert, Con 75
Colclough, Sarah 152
Cold War 82
    beginning of 83
Coleman, Marie 58
Collins Barracks, Cork 51, 107, 120, 133
    Collins Barracks Development Steering
        Group 121
Collins, Michael 3, 10, 60
    biographies of 23, 61
commemoration project funding 149
Commissioner of Public Works 20
Commonwealth
    Irish departure from 83
Coogan, Tim Pat 60, 61
Troubles, The 90

Cook, Terry 25
Cosantóir, An 91, 95, 96, 115, 126, 136, 145
    Captain Seamus Kelly Memorial
        Awards 97
Cosgrave, Liam 119
Costello, Michael 'MJ' 1, 6, 16, 22, 32, 48
Cotter, J.P.M. 35, 37
Coveney, Hugh 121
Cox, Gerard Shane 81–82
Craig, David 133
Crowe, Catriona 127, 128–129, 132, 141, 143
Cumann na mBan 58, 59, 137
Cumann na nGaedhael 13, 20
    Limerick Young Ireland Society 5
Cummins, Richard 153

Dáil Éireann 60, 95
    dramatization of first meeting 125
Daly, Liam 51, 52
Daly, Michael 89
Davis, Eugene 23
Decade of Centenaries 138, 147, 154
Deenihan, Jimmy 139
Defence Forces (Temporary Provision) Act
    (1923) 32
Defence Forces Review 136
Deignan, Joseph 69
Democratic Unionist Party (DUP) 88
Department of Arts, Sport and Tourism
    133, 134
Department of Defence 17, 133, 137
    Army Organisation Board 20
    Council of Defence 20, 29
    support for Military Archives 70
Department of Education 99, 100
Department of Finance 21, 107, 126
Department of the Taoiseach 137, 142
Derrig, Thomas 44
Destruction Order 40–1
    see also 'Burn Order'
de Valera, Éamon 21–22, 40, 44–45, 61, 126
    identity 62

de Vogel, J.C.A.J. 92
Dictionary of Irish Biography 58
Dodd, M.F. 50
Dolan, Lisa 137
Door, Noel 119
Dorney, John 61
Douglas-Home, Charles 89
Droum Ambush 49
Dublin Castle 18
 British 'War Office'
 handover to Provisional Government 10
 Irish War Office 11
 State Papers Office 7
Dublin Corporation 107
Dublin and Monaghan Bombings *see*
 McEntee Report (2007)
Duggan, John 114
Dunne, Annette 86

East Timor 145
Easter Rising (1916) 22, 59, 75
 call for reminiscences 53
Edwards, Robert Dudley 44, 126
Egan, J. 93
Emergency Powers Act 79
English, Adrian J. 115
espionage 35

Fanning, Ronan 97, 119
Ferriter, Diarmaid 128, 156
Fianna Éireann 59, 75, 137
Fianna Fáil 23, 40, 44, 139
Fisk, Robert 87, 119, 125
 In Time of War 97
FitzGerald, Desmond 13
FitzGerald, Garret 90
Flynn, Chris 134
Flynn, James 'Jimmy' 116
Fórsa Cosanta Áitiúil (FCÁ) 124
Four Courts
 shelling 61
 siege 49

Freeman's Journal 23
Frongoch (internment camp) 59
Furlong, Phil 134

Gallagher, John 100
Galvin, Thomas 2, 5–6, 13, 22, 29–31
 leaves the Army 27
Gaelic League 25
 Keating Branch 48
Garda Síochána 35, 36–37, 87, 109
 Press Office 90
General Post Office (GPO) 76
Geological Survey of Ireland 110
GHQ Papers 9, 11
Giblin, Thomas 50
Gibson, Mel 124
Gloucester jail 59
Government Buildings 18
Griffith Barracks 66, 67–68, 80
Grothier, Noelle 137, 154
Gwynn, Denis 126

Hamill, Sean 105
Harnett, Noel 77
Harrington, Niall Charles 20, 39, 40,
 48–49, 65, 67
 new appointment 79
 Volunteer Handbook of the Dublin
  Regiment 68
Harrington, Timothy 48
Harte, Frank 101
Harvey, Dan 121
Haughey, Charles J. 110
Hayes, Richard 126
Henderson, Leo 61
Henry, Frederick 32, 43
Heuston, Seán 75
Hibernian Rifles 137
Hickey, Linda 153
Higgins, Michael D. 150, 151
Historical Section Collection 42, 56, 75
Hobson, Blumer 14, 59

Hodson, Tom 58, 153
Hogan, James 126
Hopkinson, Michael 128
Humphreys, Kevin 140
Humphries, Heather 149

Institute of Public Administration 104
Intelligence Branch 1, 87, 90, 123
    GHQ 5, 13
    Press Survey Section 2
    staff expansion 2
Ireland 2016 138
Irregular Forces 3
Irish Citizen Army 137
Irish Civil War
    demobilisation 2
Irish Committee on Historical Sciences 45
Irish Defence Forces
    Congo 83
    Cyprus 83
    Directorate of Planning and Research
        92–93
    IT section 118
    official inception 32
Irish Press 23
Irish Republican Army 137
    Monaghan Brigade 43
    Sligo Brigade 59
Irish Republican Brotherhood (IRB) 49, 61
Irish Volunteers 5, 26, 59, 137
    Dublin Regiment 56
    formation 80, 126

*Journal of the Society for Army Historical
    Research* 78

Keane, Michael 137
Keaveney, Ceceila 139
Kelly, David 'Ned' 147, 152
Kelly, Patrick J. 51
Kennedy, Padraic 145, 154
Kenny, Enda 140, 148

Kenny, Henry Egan 31
Kerlin, Conor 134
Kiernan, T.J. 76
Kileen, Tony 139
Kilmainham Papers 4, 10, 78
    transfer from Operations Branch 6
Kincora Boys Home 88
Kinsella, Tony 153

Laing, Victor 104, 105, 110, 131
    posting to Bosnia 139
    retirement 144
Lawlor, Andrew 147, 152
League of Nations 82–83
Ledwige, Leanne 153
Lenihan, Brian 107, 117
Leonard, Joe 104
Leslie, Peter 115
Liberties College, Dublin 115
Libraries Papers 9, 13
Lohan, Andrew 50
Long, Pat 137
Loyalist Workers Strike (Northern
    Ireland) 87
Lucas, A.T. 99–100
Lynch Fionan 5
Lynch, Kathleen 139

Macardle, Dorothy
    Irish Republic, The 22
Mac Conmara, Tomás 154
Mac Eoin, Sean 119, 129
MacEoin, Stephen 138, 146, 152
MacEoin, Uinseann 27
    books 155–156
MacMahon, Peadar 17, 33, 63
MacMahon, Seán 14
MacNeill, Aodh 19, 75
MacNeill, Eoin 59
MacNeill, Josephine 58
MacSwiney, Mary 22
Magazine Fort 93, 101

Mahoney, Brendan 104
Manning, Maurice 122
Markham, Thomas 3, 7
    appointment by Collins 10–11
McAnally, Henry 78
McAuley, Evelyn 153
McCann, Gerry 153
McCann, Seán 140
McCarthy, Denis 114, 153
    Atari computer 116
McCarthy, Niall 113
McCarthy, Pat 112, 118–119
McCoy, John 126
McCullagh, David 61
McCullough Mulvin 150
McDermott, Joseph 152
McDermott, Seán 5
McDonald, John B. 51
McDunphy, Michael 28, 80, 126, 152
McEntee Report (2007) 37
McEvoy, Robert 137
McGrath, Mary 101
McGrath, Sam 153
McKee Barracks 18, 121
McKee, Dick 59
McKenna, Dan 79
Memorandum on the General Staff 27, 36
Memorandum to the Government on the
    Reorganisation of the Defence Forces 82
memory 51
Merrion Papers 9, 13
Michael Collins (film) 125, 130
Military Archives
    computerisation 115–116
    formal establishment 42
    government apprehension 19
    Historical Section 27, 42, 45, 46, 52
    O'Connell appointment 65–66
    outreach activities 77
    physical resourcing 120
    preparatory committee 102–103

procurement problems 69, 70, 71
proposal for 5–6, 17, 19
proposed chain of command 15, 16
reading room 133
release plans 140
re-establishment (1982) 95, 98
relocation proposal 120
research queries from abroad 123
Military Archives Oral History Project 148,
    154, 155
Military College, Curragh Camp 86, 106
Military History Society of
    Ireland 112, 118, 123
Military Heritage Trust of Ireland 123, 133
military museums
    potential 99
Military Service Pensions Act (1924) 1, 2, 3
Military Service (1916-1923) Pensions
    Collection 1, 13, 27, 43, 76, 120
    public access announcement 137
    release 142, 149
    steering committee 137, 141
Mitchell, Tom 147
Mohan, Aislinn 153
Moody, Theodore W. 126
Moore Street development 148
Moroney, Seán 51
Morrison, Eve 45, 127, 128
Mortimer, Claire 146, 152
Mulcahy, Richard 14, 28, 60
Mulvagh, Conor 144

National Archives Advisory Council 113
National Archives of Ireland 133
'thirty-year rule' 95–96
National Archives of Ireland Act (1986) 7,
    45, 76, 103–106, 137
National Army 3, 60, 137
    foundation 43
National Library of Ireland 13, 44, 53, 78, 110
National Lottery funds 117

National Museum of Ireland 35, 99, 110,
122, 133
Proclaiming a Republic 154
National Volunteers 29
No. 1 Film Support Unit 124, 130
Nowlan, P.F. 130

O'Brien, Conor Cruise 119
O'Brien, M.J. 51, 52
O'Callaghan, David 134
O'Carroll, Eamonn
Vincent 32, 42, 43–44, 48, 56
further appointments 44, 54
return to Second Bureau 57
O'Connell, J.J. 'Ginger' 29, 34, 36, 38–40,
48, 58–63, 70–71
death 80
demotion 62
kidnapping 79
recommendations and requests 71–74
O'Connell, Kathleen 22
O'Conner, Rory 61
O'Connor, C.B. 19, 29, 68, 70
O'Connor, Corán 150
Ó'Corráin, Daithí
*Colonel J.J. O'Connell's Memoir of the
Irish Volunteers, 1913–1917* 58
O'Daly, Paddy 49
O'Doherty, Brigitta 141
O'Donnell, P.D. 91
O'Donoghue, Florence 'Florrie' 126
O'Duffy, Eoin 35
Office of Public Works 133, 142
O'Halpin, Eunan 69
O'Hegarty, Diarmuid 28
O'Higgins, Seamus 37
O'Kelly, JJ 25
O'Malley, Ernie 27
Ó'Muireasáin, Seán 51
O'Neill, Jim 52
Ó Neill, P.P. 83

O'Neill, Sean 76
O'Neill, Tadgh 98
Operations Branch 2
O'Rourke, P.J. 51
Ó Snodaigh, Aengus 132
O'Sullivan, Gerald 98

Pearse Barracks 51
Pearse, Patrick 59
Portobello Barracks 13, 51
Portobello Papers 9, 13
Private Collections 9, 13
Provisional Government
Ministry of Finance 11
Public Records Office 104
destruction of 26

Queen Elizabeth I 11
Quinn, Maurice 151
Quinn, Ruairi 107

Radio Éireann 76
Reade, Brian 141
Reading Gaol 59
Red House 18, 66, 90, 95, 97
Redmond, John 29, 80
Robinson, Seamus 126
Rockwell College 86
Royal Dublin Society 69
Royal Hospital Kilmainham 3, 18, 21, 54
establishment 10
Royal Hospital Papers *see* Kilmainham
Papers
Royal Military Academy, Sandhurst 123
Royal Ulster Constabulary (RUC) 89
Russell, Charles 2
Ryan, Stephen 132, 136

Savino, Vincent 87, 92
Scéilg see O'Kelly, JJ
Schellenberg, Theodore 8

Second Bureau 33, 36, 37, 49, 63, 65
  key records 39
  Press Survey sub-section 34
  see also Intelligence Branch
Shatter, Alan 141
Sheehan, John 105
Shelbourne Hotel 89
Short, Adrian 147, 152
Sinn Féin 21, 22, 148
  Limerick Executive 5
  split 40
Slater, Fred 49
Snoddy, Oliver 100–101
State Papers Office (SPO) 104
Stein, Amelia 132
Stephens' Barracks, Kilkenny 132
Sweeney, Joseph 46, 51, 64
Swift, Jonathan 89

Teeling, Frank 55–56
Traynor, Oscar 80, 126
Trinity College Library 13
Truce (1921)
  destruction of records 109

Ulster Volunteer Force 75
United Nations 119
United Nations Emergency Force
  (UNEF) 87
United Nations Interim Force in Lebanon
  (UNIFIL) 92, 119
  Goksel, Timur 92, 106
United States
  War Department 20

United States Military Academy 123
University College Dublin 58, 123
  Diploma in Archives Studies 91, 105
  Higher Diploma in Archives 131–132
  MA in Archives and Records
    Management 136, 138, 146, 152

Volunteer Reserve Regiments 28

Wallace, Colin 88, 89
Wallace, Pat 121, 134
Walsh, George 80, 104
Wandsworth Prison 59
Weafer, Matthew 152
Whelan, Leo
  IRA GHQ Staff, 1921 59
Whelan, Michael 154–155
White, Joe 104, 112
Wolfe Tone Club 5
Woods, Seamus
World Disarmament Conference 39
World War Two 74, 79

Young, Peter 57, 77, 100–101, 104, 112, 143
  concern with Department of Defence
    attitude 108–110
  death of 128–129
  early life 86–90
  'Father of the Military Archives' 157
  legacy 129–130
  obituary 130
  PhD opportunity 119
  promotion 93